RECOLLECTIONS

OF

MY MILITARY LIFE.

BY

COLONEL LANDMANN,

LATE OF THE CORPS OF ROYAL ENGINEERS,

AUTHOR OF

"ADVENTURES AND RECOLLECTIONS," &c.

IN TWO VOLUMES.

VOL. I.

The Naval & Military Press Ltd

Published by

The Naval & Military Press Ltd
Unit 5 Riverside, Brambleside
Bellbrook Industrial Estate
Uckfield, East Sussex
TN22 1QQ England

Tel: +44 (0)1825 749494

www.naval-military-press.com
www.nmarchive.com

In reprinting in facsimile from the original, any imperfections are inevitably reproduced and the quality may fall short of modern type and cartographic standards.

PREFACE.

In laying before the public another portion of my "Recollections," I gladly avail myself of the opportunity it offers me for stating, that I had prepared a short introduction to the First Part, but which, through some mistake, was omitted, causing me all the regret which such omission was justly calculated to occasion.

I think it necessary here to state, that through the whole of the work already published, of that now about to claim the indulgence of the military world in particular, and of its further extension, which may hereafter have need of the same favour, one of my chief objects has been to make no statement which I do not firmly believe to be in strict accordance with truth. I have started with a determination to avoid that mixture of fiction with facts,—a practice which our most esteemed Historical Novelists have, with infinite talent, so profusely introduced into their admirable and most amusing works, *founded on facts.* Yet, however proud I might feel at the honour of participating, even in a slender degree, in such distinguished public favour, still I wish it to be clearly understood, that, in recording these reminiscences, I have never lost sight of my first intention.

My records are the result of memory, largely aided by voluminous documents, journals, and copious notes on the spot; and they have also been assisted by communications, carefully sifted.

I feel satisfied that my statements may be received and repeated as historical facts; my insertion of the names of interested individuals in full, should be a sufficient guarantie to that effect.

CONTENTS

OF

THE FIRST VOLUME.

CHAPTER I.

The Loyal Briton—Persons that embark—Officers' names —Dirty state of the Ship and no Medical Officers— Mrs. McSheen—Departure for Gibraltar—An immense Fleet—A scene of Confusion—The cocked hat—Fair weather—Coast of Portugal. . . . 1

CHAPTER II.

A gallant defence against pirates—Berlingas—Rock of Lisbon—A man falls overboard—Cape San Vicente— Changing our course—Cape Spartel—Precautions on approaching the Straits—Magnificent scenery—Trafalgar—Barroza—Tarrifa—Some danger from privateers and gun-boats—Apollo—Anchor at Gibraltar . 16

CHAPTER III.

Lieutenant-Colonel Fyers—Great rise in the temperature—First night on Shore—A severe Fall—Scorpion bite—Flowers on top of House—Mrs. Fox nearly drowned—A Wedding — The Minorca — Sir Sidney Smith at General Fox's—His mode of Defence with a Dirk against a Cutlass—Races—The Earl of Northesk, and my impudence 32

CHAPTER IV.

Parties and Excursions—Catland Bay—Pelted by the Monkeys—Party to St. George's Hall—Magnificent Scenery—Narrow escape from an immense stone hurled at us by the Monkeys—Ride about with General Fox—The Devil's Bowling-Green—Military Garden—Sir Joseph Banks and the Gloucestershire Prophet 48

CHAPTER V.

I request to be employed on actual service—Press General Fox to take me to Sicily with him—Edward Ellers, of the Navy—Sharp repartee, and loss of the Arrow—Take leave of Ellers—Kick up a row with the dogs—All's well—Kilvington—Alarm the fleet—General Fox and family sail away to Messina . 62

CONTENTS. vii

CHAPTER VI.

General Drummond assumes the command—Excursions —War on the water and peace on land—General Castaños—Lieutenant Blaquier, R.N.—Amateur Theatricals—Pizarro—Doctor O'Rorke takes his leave of the stage 77

CHAPTER VII.

The great powder-magazine in danger of blowing-up— The Author had already saved another powder magazine from blowing-up at Quebec—Blue Peter— Monkey caught in the act—Witness a bull-fight— Narrow escape 91

CHAPTER VIII.

The Orion returns from Messina—The Author consents to dine on board with Ellers—The torture he endured —Danger of being carried off to Sea—The difficulty of escaping from the Orion—Landing from a launch —Rozia Bay—Rather queer sort of work, but ultimate escape 111

CHAPTER IX.

The 13th of September—Floating Batteries—Rejoicings on this Anniversary—St. Michael's Cave—Loss of the Athenian, a very authentic account—Lieutenant-General Sir Hew Dalrymple arrived—The Marquis and Marchioness of Santa Cruz, Colonel Stirling, and

viii   CONTENTS.

Bagpipes—Mr. Wilson, a Jeweller from Lisbon—A
Topaz Suite for an English Countess—The Countess
de Noailles—Major Bryce 134

CHAPTER X.

Change quarters—Good garden—Colonel Fyers tries the
change of air by going to sea with Sir George Cockburn, and finally goes to England—The Royal George,
Sir I. T. Duckworth—Very polite reception of my
visit—Stone shot and Maltese ass—The 6th Regiment
arrived—Toss-up Toledano, a celebrated Jew . 156

CHAPTER XI.

Bottles of Porter concealed—O'Hara in a difficulty—
His various efforts to detect negligence in the military
duty—Party to Algeziras hastily terminated—Spanish
Marquis and the celebrated Marotti—A very unpleasant affair 172

CHAPTER XII.

The night-blowing cereus rather expensive property,
and very shameful behaviour of the company—The
ghost of Lieutenant Hunter of the 42nd Regiment—
Attacked with cholera. 195

CHAPTER XIII.

The Garden Fête, good, but bad—The Prospects of a
Siege—His Excellency Mr. Elliot—The Garrison is
blockaded—Sir Charles Holloway arrives—Increased
Forces arrive—Silver Spoons—Prices greatly aug-

CONTENTS. ix

mented—Sir John Moore—General Beresford occupied Madeira—Speculations on the intended operations—Occupation of the Island of Perexil and its advantages—Major Burk—Ceuta is supposed to be the object of attack—The Author volunteers his services to Sir Charles Holloway to serve in any Expedition, and so does Mercer . . . 212

CHAPTER XIV.

Very suddenly ordered to embark—Attend to the shipping of the stores—Captain Morrison appointed to embark to command the Artillery — Lieutenant Mercer and myself embark—Departure from Gibraltar with an East wind sometimes more difficult than might be expected—The guitar . . . 228

CHAPTER XV.

Active speculations as to the destination of the expedition —Join the fleet off Cadiz—Sir John Gore fired upon, while carrying a flag of truce—General Spencer as Lieutenant-Colonel commanding the 40th Regiment on landing in Egypt—Frequent intercourse with the fishing boats—Profitable trade carried on off Cadiz— Catching whales no joke 241

CHAPTER XVI.

Lord Amelius Beauclerk and his little Terrible—Cape Flyaway—The Spanish fishing boats—A row on board the Admiral—The author has a narrow escape of being shot in mistake 259

CHAPTER XVII.

Prayers by the Chaplain—Flags of Truce—Mr. Collison—Captain Maxwell—Come to Anchor—Anxiety in regard to our Prospects—Conflicting Information—Signal for Adjutants—A Big Bundle of Boards—Our Skipper in a Stew—Go to Sea again—John Bull—Off towards Gibraltar—All our Hopes crushed—Recalled and sent back to the Fleet—Expectation of Disembarking—Disappointment—Anniversary of the Birth of George the Third—Sir John Gore and Sir George Smith—Marquis of Solana . . 272

CHAPTER XVIII.

The ships of War anchor outside of the Transports—The Alceste goes to England with some Officers of the English and Spanish Armies—Lord Collingwood invites me to Dinner—Midshipman Festing dines at the Admiral's table also—Lord Collingwood's wit—General Spencer—I go on Shore, well received—I meet some old Friends—I receive some very kind presents of Provision—The Attack of the Ships belonging to Villeneuve's Squadron is commenced—The San José suffers no injury—The San José disabled—I go to Fort Luis—I am sent for by the Spanish Admiral, and requested to go to Collingwood for Powder—The 6th Regiment and some Artillery arrive from Gibraltar—The Spanish Officers account for not sinking the French Ships, ... 287

RECOLLECTIONS

OF

MY MILITARY LIFE.

CHAPTER I.

The Loyal Briton—Persons that embark—Officers' names—Dirty state of the Ship and no Medical Officers—Mrs. McSheen—Departure for Gibraltar—An immense Fleet—A scene of Confusion—The cocked hat—Fair weather—Coast of Portugal.

THE Loyal Briton transport, in which I was ordered to embark for Gibraltar, arrived at Portsmouth from Woolwich, in December, 1805, having experienced a boisterous and tedious passage of many weeks' duration, for there were in those days no steamers to brave the storms and tides, and so determine the length of such voyages within a limited number of hours. This ship had already received on board at Woolwich large detachments of the Royal Artillery and Royal Military Artificers (now Sappers and Miners), appointed to proceed to Gibraltar, in order to replace the immense losses those corps had sustained, by the ravages of a sort of yellow fever, which had raged there with awful severity during that Summer and Autumn, and which had, in the course of a few weeks, swept away exactly one half of the two companies of the Royal Military Artificers stationed in that fortress, then three hundred men strong.

With these troops, from seventy to eighty women, and nearly as many children, had been shipped; so that, including the officers and the ship's company, the total number of persons crammed into that transport amounted to about four hundred.

The names of the officers embarked, were; of the Royal Artillery, Captains Francis Smith and John Fead, and Lieutenants Kane, Heron, and Robinson; those of the Royal Engineers were, Captains Henry Evatt (the senior officer on board) and myself, and Lieutenants George Judd Harding and Henry Mulcaster. Lieutenant Cavalier Shorthose Mercer was ordered to proceed to Gibraltar at the same time, but he had the good fortune to obtain a passage on board the Pompey, Admiral Sir Sidney Smith, and he joined us at Gibraltar, shortly after our arrival there.

About the middle of January, 1806, I embarked on board the Loyal Briton, of four hundred tons burthen, then lying at anchor on the Mother-bank. We soon discovered that the young and inexperienced officers, to whom the troops had been entrusted from Woolwich to Portsmouth, had entirely neglected the cleaning between decks, through which so much filth had accumulated, that it is astonishing we escaped typhus fever. It is a positive fact, that a great number of the women and children had not once quitted their beds, during more than six weeks prior to this period ; in consequence of which, much difficulty was now experienced, in compelling them to rise at eight o'clock every morning, and remain on deck during a few hours, whilst the operation of scraping and fumigating between decks should be carried into effect. Indeed, so determined were many of the women to resist this salutary and indispensable measure, that they opposed force to force.

On one occasion, when I was on duty between decks, superintending the levee of those ladies, a Mrs. McSheen manifested a strong determination to resist the order for adjournment to the deck. At first she was very ill, and described her sufferings, with a pure Tipperary accent, as proceeding from a pain all over her, and a smothering about her heart; she then had entirely lost the use of her legs. These complaints were, however, disregarded, and she was peremptorily informed that no such excuse could save her from making her appearance forthwith on the deck. Upon this, Mrs. McSheen most energetically declared that no power upon earth should move her from that place; "neither officer, non-commissioned officer, nor private soldier," had a right to interfere with her; and, in order to add force and solemnity to this determination, she wound up with the closing words of an oath.

Having thus expressed her unalterable declaration, Mrs. McSheen rolled her eyes about her to detect, if possible, the effect it might have produced on the by-standers; but she was immediately relieved from her anxiety by hearing the order repeated. Her blood was now up, and she replied, with a running fire of the most elegant extracts, interspersed with an occasional well-directed stick, old shoe, decayed potatoe, and many nameless etceteras, with which she pelted all those around her. This proving ineffectual, Mrs. McSheen had now recourse to the only remaining untried expedient; she, accordingly, screamed most violently five or six times, leaving appropriate spaces of time betwixt each, then roared out, " murther!—murther!—murther!" and quickly fainted away. Such an opportunity was not to be neglected; I quickly ordered two or three men, together with private McSheen, of the Royal Military Artificers, her husband, to carry her upon deck, and there give her the benefit of a bucket-full of water. The men stepped forward with alacrity; but Mrs. Mc Sheen having a great objection to cold water, in the most deliberate manner raised herself up to a sitting posture. We all stood back, expecting a renewal of hostilities, in some improved and more desperate form; nothing, however, could have been further from her thoughts; with a countenance most serene, yet full of dignity, she gracefully quitted her couch, advanced with measured step, and joined the other women upon deck without uttering a single word.

After some days, matters went on more smoothly; but, as we had no surgeon on board, our situation was truly alarming, especially when it is remembered, that four hundred persons, a large portion of whom were women and children, had already been embarked a long time, and that several weeks might still elapse before we should sail, through the frequent delays experienced when proceeding with convoys, to which must be added a sea voyage of a fortnight or three weeks at least, before we could expect to reach our destination. These facts induced Captain Evatt to remonstrate officially against our departure without the aid of a medical officer. I do not now recollect the excuse made or reason assigned for not granting so just a demand; but I perfectly remember that we all considered ourselves most shamefully treated.

Whilst we were still lying at anchor at the Mother-bank, we experienced some very severe gales, particularly on Saturday, the 18th of January, the day on which the anniversary of the Queen's birth was then celebrated. Towards mid-day we were on the look-out for the salutes from the King's ships of war, when we observed a Portsmouth wherry, containing four women passengers, tacking, and beating to windward, in order to reach some ship near us; but suddenly, in passing under our stern, the boat was upset. The watermen swam well, and, fortunately, the clothes of the women floated them, until they were rescued.

During several weeks previous to this time, the almost daily arrival of small fleets under convoys from various parts of our Eastern coasts, greatly augmented the already enormous accumulation of shipping preparing to depart for every quarter of the globe, so soon as proper convoys should be appointed.

At length, on the 28th of January, 1806, a beautifully fine morning, with a light breeze from the Eastward, the much-desired and so-long-expected signal was made, and in the course of a few hours eight hundred to nine hundred merchant vessels spread their white sails, and were seen gliding majestically in various directions, as guided by the signals floating in the wind on the lofty masts of the convoying ships, which occasionally fired a cannon to procure a more active attention from the vessels under their respective charge. Our position was nearly central; and so dense was this vast crowd of moving canvass, that our view of the shore and of the horizon was at times almost totally eclipsed.

The gradual collection and simultaneous departure of such an immense fleet would now very probably attract many thousands of spectators, even from distant parts; yet in those days no one travelled a single mile out of his way, to witness this splendid display of the maritime wealth of Great Britain.

Whilst we proceeded towards the Needles, a large portion of this enormous fleet were observed to be following their convoying ships round St. Helens, to pass outside of the Isle of Wight; and the daylight had nearly left us when we reached the British Channel. During the night our progress was frequently checked, in order that the dullest sailing ships might have time to join the others,—an annoyance continually experienced when sailing with convoys. As the sun rose, throwing over us its menacing red glare, we discovered that six ships of the line, and a vast number of frigates and smaller armed vessels, had been appointed to protect us against the enemy's cruizers.

The peaceful smoothness of the sea was of short duration; our fair wind down channel was followed by a succession of severe gales from the South-west, which continued unabated during twelve to fourteen days. On various occasions we had an opportunity of noticing that the larger ships, particularly those of the line, such as the St. George, a three-decker, seemed to suffer quite as much, nay, I believe, more than we did. At one time we were within two hundred yards of that ship, when we could perceive how severely she laboured, and that she frequently plunged her bows completely under water. During the whole of this period we made but little progress towards our destination. Deprived of every comfort, we were thankful that we could still obtain the most urgent necessities, since, during three days, such had been the severity of the gales, that it had been found impossible to cook any article of provision; and not without great perseverance had we occasionally managed to boil a small quantity of water on the cabin fire.

On the second day after our departure, when I was seated at one end of the dinner-table which had been placed across the ship, with my back against the cabins, the ship was rolling more than usual, and every one at the same moment catching hold of the table to save himself from sliding with violence to leeward, for the seats were not fastened, it suddenly gave way, and I do believe it would have cut me into two pieces just below my ribs, had I not with great activity slipped aside. I now darted towards the cabin door, and had the good fortune to get into its opening, where I could hold fast, and where I beheld such a mass of confusion as beggars all description. I shall merely state, that about a dozen persons were on the floor, rolling from side to side, catching at everything and at one another. I saw one in particular most obstinately embracing a chair, with which he had thrown several summersets before he discovered his error. A tureen of soup, with a boiled goose in it, and a large dish of potatoes, were actively making their way over the company on the floor, who, in their turn, were pulverizing the plates, dishes, decanters, glasses, &c., in fine style.

In the midst of this chaos, as if in order that nothing should be wanting to render the work of destruction as complete as possible, an eighteen-gallon cask of table-beer, about the fastening of which much time and industry had been expended, broke from all its ordinary and extraordinary lashings, and commenced its destructive revolutions from bulkhead to bulk-head, bounding from the back of one on to the legs of another, expelling shrieks and groans from all whom it so particularly favoured; but it had not thus promenaded more than twice the width of the cabin, when the brass cock was displaced, upon which the swipes spurted out in circular movement, as it irrigated the terrified sufferers sprawling on the floor. I was the only one out of danger; and it would have been impossible to calculate the extent of personal injuries which might have been inflicted in a few minutes by this tremendous smashing machine, had not a favourable opportunity presented itself by a temporary lull that enabled me to arrest its further progress, by turning it up briskly on one of its ends, and with the utmost exertion I succeeded in drawing it into the lobby.

To my infinite surprise, no serious injuries had been sustained by any one, though all had received abundance of scratches and bruises.

In a few days after this, Lieutenant Kane, of the Royal Artillery, having a superlative cocked-hat, in a flat case made to fit, which he very imperfectly fastened to the outside of the bulk-head of his cabin, it broke loose, and during the whole of the night tumbled about the cabin floor, to our great annoyance, depriving the majority of us of rest. On the following morning, I strongly remonstrated with the proprietor, urging the necessity of adopting a more perfect mode of fastening his hat-box, which he promised to carry into effect, but which was performed with no better success, for during the next night the hat and box again dropped from the partition, and we, as before, were deprived of rest. There was evidently much carelessness in thus manifesting a total disregard of our comfort; and, in order to induce the owner to prevent the recurrence of such a nuisance, I said to him that if he did not most effectually fasten his three-cornered scraper, I should do it myself in a very efficient manner, by driving the largest spike-nail I could procure in the ship through both hat and box.

Notwithstanding this powerful appeal to his affectionate feelings towards this exclusive hat, that night the box came down again; and next morning, without mentioning my intention to any one, I obtained a large spike from the ship's carpenter, which I cut in two, at about two inches from the head. I then, but not without considerable labour, filed a point to the stump having the head, and by forming a shoulder, so that when this thin point was driven, or rather merely pushed with the hand into the soft deal box, it would exactly have the appearance of a spike of large dimensions driven through hat and all, to within an inch of the head.

A favourable opportunity, when no one happened to be in the cabin, enabled me to push or press this harmless spike up to the shoulder into the middle of the box, without, however, piercing the thin wood of which it was made. In a few minutes the owner and others came down from the deck, and no great length of time passed before it was observed.

On perceiving that such irreparable injury had been done to the most perfect, the most knowing, and the most exquisite hat ever made by Bicknell, his feelings were, as may be easily imagined, excited to the utmost degree. He vented his ire without reserve, declaring that no rank nor any other circumstance should protect the perpetrator of such a shameful act

—— ; it was a deed which he never could forget, and which he never would forgive.

His rage having reached to the highest pitch, he seized the poker, with a full determination to demolish the box, if necessary, in order to tear it off from the bulkhead, to which, as he thought, it was so firmly attached; and then, who knows what would have been the next use he would have made of the poker, had not the first touch caused the head of the spike to fall down, and thus suddenly disclosed to the enraged proprietor the imposture which had been so successfully practised on him.

At length, as the sailors say, "after the storm comes the calm," we had moderate weather, the wind not contrary, and the sea less agitated, which in a few days enabled us to reach the coast of Portugal.

CHAPTER II.

A gallant defence against pirates—Berlingas—Rock of Lisbon—A man falls overboard—Cape San Vicente—Changing our course—Cape Spartel—Precautions on approaching the Straits—Magnificent scenery—Trafalgar—Barroza—Tarrifa—Some danger from privateers and gun-boats—Apollo—Anchor at Gibraltar.

From this moment we adopted greater vigilance during the night, as we had heard that many British merchant ships had been captured and plundered by privateers and pirates, who frequented the Bay of Vigo in particular; and the latter, who were chiefly from Algiers or Salee, rarely showed any mercy.

Amongst these stories, our skipper related one which made a deep impression on my memory, and was nearly as follows: "It is not more than about five years ago that a British merchantman bound to the Mediterranean, was becalmed just within sight of the land, nearly on the same spot that we now occupy; and in the course of a few hours two large galleys were observed from the ship, rowing with all their might and main towards it.

"The Captain, an old and experienced navigator in those parts, very soon understood their intention; but without guns, and with only thirty-three hands on board, ill provided with muskets, it was more easy to determine on resistance than to devise the means of successfully carrying it into effect; for, failure after such an attempt would place them in a far worse position than tame surrender. Having formed his plan, the Captain called his men aft, and with a pompous step ascended the poop, when he began by turning up the front part of an old foul-weather hat, which had been covered and recovered with painted canvass, some dozen of times or more, and then brandishing his spyglass, he pointed to the suspicious-looking boats. After remaining a short while in this attitude, he began.—' I say, my lads, do you see them air ugly, black-looking fellers—they are what we calls piruts—if you don't fight for it, they'll cut up and pickle some on us, and sarve it out to the Christian slaves in Africa, as a treat on holidays; and the rest they'll make over as a feast for the sharks, as you sees there sailing about the ship; but if they should happen to be in a particular kind-hearted way, then we shall be carried away to Barbary, and made to hatch eggs for the Emperor of Morocco, or the Dey of Algiers.—I say, let us fight it out, and take our chance; as for me, I'd just as soon be knocked on the head at onst, as be turned into a clucking hen for all the rest of my life.—I say, mind what I tells you—and do as I bids you, and sure as the North-star, we'll beat 'em off—and I shouldn't mind laying a new trumpet we take one on 'em and sink the tother!!'

"The effect which this powerful appeal produced on the young sailors went home to their hearts, which they manifested by loud and continued cheering, whilst the hats swung round and round; and they at once declared they would stand by each other like Britons.

"The Captain," continued our skipper, "now looked big, and assumed an air of mystery and extraordinary severity. He soon afterwards went below, and returned followed by the cabin boy and steward, each of them carrying half-a-dozen empty, old-fashioned, square Dutch gin bottles, every one of them capable of containing three pints or more of liquid. These were carefully ranged and secured on one side of the deck near the gangway, and a like number were brought up and deposited in a similar manner on the opposite side of the ship. A couple of barrels of gunpowder were then opened, and the bottles carefully filled from the same. As many pieces of slow match, each about three inches long, and as many as there were bottles, then were cut and stuck into the bottles' necks, and made to fit very tight. Having completed these arrangements, all the old muskets, about forty in number, were supplied with new flints, and loaded with two balls cut into slugs, and to each man ten cartridges were delivered. They now boldly awaited the rapid advance of the pirates, without allowing them to discover the slightest intention of resistance.

"Every man was now ordered to sit down and conceal himself behind the bulwarks, the Captain alone walking the deck with his eyes almost constantly directed on the gallies, which were coming down upon them in fine style, within half-a-mile of the ship.

"With the aid of his spy-glass he clearly distinguished the gallies were as full of turbaned heads as they could hold. Not a sound disturbed the silence which now prevailed, excepting the occasional flapping of a stay-sail, as the vessel rolled from side to side, and the creaking of the bulkheads below. Amidst this awful state of suspense the Captain gruffly called out, 'Steward,' 'Ay—ay—sir,' was echoed from the cabin, whence the steward instantly popped up his head. 'Sarve out a full allowance of one-water grog all round, do you hear, sir?' 'Ay—ay—sir.' 'B equick.' 'Ay—ay—sir,' was the steward's reply; and he was on deck with the stuff before you could have said 'Jack Robinson.'

"Whilst this order was being carried into effect, the Captain hummed to himself the well-known sea-song, 'Hearts of Oak are our ships,' &c.; and amused himself by lighting the slow matches hanging out of the bottles, which, by the time the enemy could reach the ship, would have formed a strong red cinder, without burning so far as to endanger a premature explosion.

"In a few minutes more the boats were along side of the ship, one at each gangway, upon which the Captain gave the word 'Now for it, my boys!' which had been previously arranged should be the signal for jumping up, and for each man to seize a bottle and cast it with all his strength into the nearest galley. The bottles were thus smashed to pieces, and the lighted matches coming in contact with the gunpowder, which had spread over the men as well as over the bottom of the boat, produced a succession of explosions, and which not only killed an immense number of the pirates, but threw them into the greatest confusion and consternation; many of them jumping overboard into the sea, to extinguish the flames of their light dresses.

"The Captain on the poop observing the happy result of his defence, called out to his men, 'Now, my brave fellers, take to your muskets, and pick out to your liking, but mind, don't spare none on 'em!' The Captain was obeyed, and although the gallies succeeded ultimately in effecting a retreat, no doubt those who escaped, being wounded by shot, were almost to a man dreadfully scorched by the exploding gunpowder thrown amongst them, and which had been materially increased by the blowing-up of their own ammunition."

The ingenuity and boldness of the Captain, in defending his ship successfully, against such unequal odds, excited our highest admiration; and we frequently afterwards jested on the possibility of our being at no distant date engaged in leading a sedentary life, hatching eggs in the garret of the Emperor of Morocco, or the Dey of Algiers.

The first land we made was the Berlingas, or Borlings, a group of rocks and a small island, with a fort garrisoned by a serjeant and twenty men, distant about twelve miles Westward from the peninsular of Peniche. Here we had a most delightful run along the coast; a very agreeable change in the temperature had also taken place; the wind quite fair from the North-West, and the sea nearly smooth. The view of the palace of Mafra, five or six miles inland from the coast, and seated on a commanding range of hills, was very interesting.

Before nightfall we passed the Rock of Lisbon, with its sharp-pointed pinnacles, evidently of volcanic origin, and rising into the blue sky, about two thousand five hundred feet above the sea; and whence, on the north side of the entrance to the Tagus, extends a long projecting piece of sandy and flat land, with a lighthouse on its extreme advance into the sea, and which is the most Western spot in all Europe, called Cape Roca.

On the following day, the ship, with as much canvass as we could display, was scudding away towards Cape San-Vicente (St. Vincent), at the rate of nine knots per hour,

and we all sat down to dinner in high spirits;
but, just as I was inserting my knife into an
apple-pie, we suddenly heard a general confusion on deck,—all the people running aft,
and a loud cry of "A man overboard!" sounded
from stem to stern.

In a moment we were all on deck. I
hastily looked about for something that would
float, and instantly observed the drum, on
which the Roast-beef-of-old-England had been
beaten to call us to dinner, I threw it overboard, as far astern as I could, although I
was unable to see the poor fellow in the water;
and many other articles were in like manner
hurriedly disposed of.

A quarter of an hour was now unavoidably
consumed in shortening sail, before it could be
safe or even possible to let down the boat,
that was suspended under the stern. Captain
John Fead, of the Royal Artillery, then most
gallantly jumped into her, and with four
sailors was lowered into the sea, under circumstances of considerable risk, for the ship's
way had not yet been quite stopped. Fead
pushed off, and rowed about in every direction

in a much rougher sea than we had perceived or suspected, whilst going before the wind; the quantity of pieces of wood, hen-coops, casks, &c., which had been thrown to the unfortunate man instantly after he had fallen into the water, sufficiently guided him to the vicinity of the spot where the man might still be found, if able to float; but after more than an hour's fruitless endeavours, the boat returned.

Just at the moment when this man fell overboard, a frigate, one of our convoy, was close astern of us, and we hailed her, and made every effort in our power to induce her to assist in saving the man; and we had the additional distress of seeing her pass within a hundred and fifty yards of us on our larboard side, without noticing our hailing or our signals.

The man had been sitting on the gunwale, near the starboard bow, with the fore-sheet under his knees, which, in consequence of going before the wind, was hanging quite slack, although subject to rise up very suddenly, with a powerful jerk, by the flapping of the fore-sail, which the motion of the vessel or partial flurry of the wind might occasion. I had noticed the danger to which this man was exposed, and had warned him of the consequences, upon which he had changed his position; but, on my leaving the deck, I was informed he resumed his former seat, which, in a few minutes later, cost him his life.

The apple-pie—the first we had had since our embarcation—had been frequently mentioned between breakfast and dinner, and no doubt had passed through the minds of many of us still more frequently; yet, now it was put away whole and unbroken. No one had any appetite left. During the remainder of the day, and several days following, our conversation could not be diverted from the fatal event we had all witnessed; and which, on me, made an impression so deep and lasting, that, for many years afterwards, the whole of this tragical scene would force itself on my recollection, and would frequently pass and repass before my eyes in the most vivid and truthful colours.

The same steady breeze, from the Northward, carried us on to Cape San-Vicente, the most

Southern and Western land of Europe; and we had calculated that, beyond this point, although our course would be changed from nearly due South to nearly due East, the wind from the same point of the compass, N.W., would still be fair, and that in less than a couple of days we should enter the Straits of Gibraltar in fine style. However, on reaching the Cape, to our mortification, we discovered that the wind was thence direct in our teeth from the Eastward; and I was afterwards informed, that whenever the wind is from the North or North-West on the Western coast of Portugal, the wind at the same time is from the Eastward on the Southern coast. On several subsequent occasions, when I sailed round this Cape, and when I afterwards travelled along the coast on horse-back, the truth of this was confirmed.

Having run to the Southward a few leagues beyond the Cape, we directed our course towards the East; and although the wind was quite contrary, we soon passed Cape Spartel, the North-West angle of Africa.

In approaching the Straits, we thought it

advisable to put all our fighting tools in the best condition; the muskets were supplied with new flints, and the soldiers with twenty rounds of ball-cartridge per man, and the six twelve-pounder carronades on deck were overhauled and loaded with canister, and all their implements inspected, and side-arms put in order and ready for a stout resistance, until some of the vessels of war could come to our rescue.

The wind was still moderate from the Eastward, rendering it necessary to beat to windward through the Straits; but, as the current is constantly running into the Mediterranean, the dullest sailing vessel will always accomplish that operation with ease; and a contrary wind in this situation should be hailed with satisfaction by the lovers of magnificent scenery, since, through the necessity of tacking from side to side of the Straits, much nearer views of the two shores are obtained than would be the case with a fair wind; and we are thus rewarded beyond the power of the most lively description.

Soon after passing Cape Spartel on our

right, the indraught of the Mediterranean was very perceptible, and we could not fail being greatly interested with the view of the brilliantly white houses of Tangiers and their flat roofs, forming an admirable contrast with the rich colouring of the surrounding country. As we proceeded, the prospects on our right were truly sublime; the high mountains of the African coast ascending from the very margin of the sea, in endless forms, broken, and in some places totally separated from each other by frightful chasms; the magnificent forests covering large tracts of sheltered valleys, bounded by gigantic precipices of naked rock, towering high up into the deep blue sky, formed on every tack a variety of the grandest scenery that it is possible to imagine.

Although the beauties of the Northern or Spanish side would have claimed our most active interest, had it not been eclipsed by the magnificence of the African coast; yet, in addition to the truly splendid pictures which it presented at every hour, it called to our happy recollection the never-fading lustre of Nelson's name, as we passed the low Cape of Trafalgar. Then, still further, the view of the ground, although imperfect, upon which the battle of Barroza was fought in 1811, where the united British, Hanoverian, and Portuguese troops gained a victory at a dreadful sacrifice of human blood, will call forth our pride not unmixed with sorrow; but in passing the town of Tarrifa, simply walled round, the gallant and absolutely heroic defence of that place by the British troops, a mere handful of men, under the brave Colonel Skerret, will again warm our hearts.

When still about eighteen miles from the termination of our voyage, by which time the greater part of our fleet, with the convoying men-of-war, had nearly entered the bay of Gibraltar, we observed a privateer and five gun-boats come out of Tarrifa, making the utmost efforts to attack us. This was no pleasant sight, for these vessels carried a large number of men and long heavy guns, with which they might sink us without coming within the range of our carronades. Fortunately, however, the Apollo frigate, observing their movements, hastened to our rescue, upon which the enemy gave up the chase.

In running for the Bay of Gibraltar, we passed sufficiently close to the Spanish battery on Cabrita Point, to be saluted with a few shots; but they politely ranged far above and beyond our ship; and in a couple of hours later, just as the sun was sinking below the horizon, we were snug at anchor, under the walls of Gibraltar.

The view of Gibraltar from the anchorage is exceedingly interesting, particularly to Johnny Newcome, about to take up his quarters at that place. The name, *Rock* of Gibraltar, presents to our imagination a huge black or brown mass, thinly scattered over with stunted and burnt-up plants; we were, therefore, most agreeably surprised at beholding the rich vegetation so profusely intermixed with variously coloured buildings, extending from the fortification along the sea, to a considerable way up the face of the mountain, where, in many places, we observed long scarlet lines like regiments of soldiers, which afterwards we discovered to be hedges of geraniums in full bloom.

CHAPTER III.

Lieutenant-Colonel Fyers—Great rise in the temperature—First night on Shore—A severe Fall—Scorpion bite—Flowers on top of House—Mrs. Fox nearly drowned—A Wedding — The Minorca — Sir Sidney Smith at General Fox's—His mode of Defence with a Dirk against a Cutlass—Races—The Earl of Northesk, and my impudence.

As soon as the morning gun had been fired from the top of the rock on the following day, we were surrounded by bum-boats offering fruits and vegetables in great variety, with numerous other articles of consumption; and then also came Billy Pratique (William Sweetland, Esq.), the Pratique master, who, having received satisfactory answers to two or three questions, a mere form as regarded vessels from Great Britain, he granted us leave to have intercourse with the Gibraltarians.

Captain Evatt, our chief, now landed (Sunday, the 23rd of February, 1806), to report our arrival; and returned with an order from Lieutenant-Colonel William Fyers, the commanding Royal-Engineer, to disembark the officers and men of the corps, and, at the same time, delivered an invitation for the officers of Engineers to dine with him. Having made my arrangements regarding my baggage, I took leave of Mr. Heath, the Master of the Loyal Briton, and proceeded to the shore, where I was much surprised, at this early period of the year, to find on landing so great a change in the temperature. Whilst on the water, the climate was agreeably cool; but immediately on arriving within a few yards of the landing-place called Ragged-Staff, we felt a rise in the temperature of some fifteen to twenty degrees at least.

The kind and obliging reception we experienced from our truly worthy new commandant, Lieutenant-Colonel William Fyers, fully maintained his far-famed reputation for amiability of disposition and liberal hospitality, in which Mrs. Fyers and daughters kindly contributed their best efforts. At an early hour after dinner, we were permitted to retire, in order to make the best arrangements in our power for passing the night in our quarters, which our commandant had taken care should be repaired and cleaned prior to our arrival. Before midnight, I had not only set up my folding bedstead, but my bed-room furniture was completely arranged; and, moreover, my mosquito curtains were in their place, the luxury of luxuries in a warm or hot climate, and might be a very agreeable protection against the annoyance of the music and bites of the gnats, and also of the common black flies.

The house allotted to me was in South-Port Street, nearly opposite to the South Storehouse, and Captain Evatt was put in possession of a very good house adjoining the South side of mine. In a couple of days, I made my quarters comfortable, but I deeply regretted having no kind of garden. However, in order to provide a substitute, although a very humble one, I filled some of the packing-cases I had brought from England with earth, and located them on the roof of an outbuilding. In these I planted a great number of tuberoses, and abundance of orange seeds ; to these I daily added such indigenous plants as I collected in my rambles on the rock, particularly the orchis, of which I procured a variety. In a short time, I had the satisfaction of seeing my tube-roses in blossom, and send forth a most fragrant perfume ; my orange trees shot up at a surprising rate.

I narrowly escaped, however, paying very dearly for this innocent amusement; for my garden being elevated about eleven feet above the yard, my only communication with it was by a ladder, whence I could water, cultivate, and admire. By degrees, I suppose, I became careless in placing the ladder, when, on one occasion, in carrying up a vessel of water in one hand, and a new plant in the other, away I went sideways with the ladder to the ground, when I fell with my left elbow on the flint paving. I was fortunate in not breaking a single bone, but I received several severe bruises, and the tip bone of my left elbow was split, and so it now remains.

In the course of the same day my servant was stung in the wrist by a scorpion, which produced a considerable swelling of the arm, as high as the shoulder.

In addition to the cultivation of flowers, I occasionally amused myself in polishing the various specimens of lime-stone of which the rock is composed, and particularly some very handsome blocks of petrified water, which are found in large masses of broken stalactites, at the back or Eastern side of the rock. Of this material various articles are made, from the common paper weights, ink-stands, &c., to the full sized punch-bowl and chimney-pieces.

I was proceeding one day to the back of the rock in search of a large piece of the petrified water; and on reaching a little bay preceding Catland-Bay, with a narrow sandy beach, hemmed-in by rocks, I met General Fox's family returning, in consequence of Mrs. Fox having been nearly drowned, in attempting to cross that bay, by a wave which

MY MILITARY LIFE. 37

had swept her into the sea; and it was with great difficulty, and considerable personal risk to himself, that Captain Young, the General's Aide-de-Camp, had, by rushing into the sea, been able to save her; as both were several times carried backwards and forwards before Captain Young could regain and secure his footing.

On my return home I received an invitation to pass the evening at Major-General Smith's, the commanding officer of Artillery, to be present at the marriage ceremony, by special licence, of his daughter, with Lieutenant Buchannan, of the Royal Engineers. Accordingly, on the 11th of March, having made myself smart for the occasion, I proceeded to the General's house, near the Spanish church, and there met a large party, amongst whom were General and Mrs. Drummond, and Miss Read, Mrs. Drummond's sister; General and Mrs. Gross, and their son; Mrs. Jephson, sister of the bride, and Mr. Jephson; Colonel and Mrs. Fyers, and Miss Fyers, of the Royal Engineers; Brigade-Major Patrick Campbell, and Lieutenant Cameron, of the Royal Artillery; and perhaps some others. Both the bride and bridegroom were of delicate constitution and health, and the former was exceedingly pretty; both of them died of consumption, leaving a numerous family.

At twenty minutes before eight o'clock the garrison chaplain, Mr. Hughes, an aged and most excellent man, rose, and having arranged the company as he wished them to stand, the ceremony, a very short one, was immediately performed; and on its conclusion the gentlemen, excepting Mr. Gross, a young gentleman not more than sixteen or seventeen years of age, saluted the whole of the ladies, each commencing with the bride.

The bride, perceiving the *mauvaise honte* of young Gross, now made a very spirited attempt, encouraged by all the company, on Mr. Gross, who, nevertheless, with extraordinary activity, succeeded in saving his cheek from the intended violence.

This, of course, produced a great deal of mirth and merriment, and the remainder of the evening was passed most agreeably.

The absence of Colonel Keane (since then,

Lord Keane) and Mrs. Keane was frequently mentioned with regret by all the individuals of the party; but pressing matters had compelled them to sail for England, on the 1st of March, in the Britannia. Mrs. Keane was also a daughter of General Smith's.

I had nearly omitted to mention the amiable Julia Smith, the youngest daughter of the General, who was at that time very young, but even then gave the strongest assurances of possessing that degree of beauty for which she has since been so justly celebrated. She was soon after this married to a Mr. Baines, of Canton, and has resided in China for many years.

The climate of Gibraltar at this period of the year was most delightful, and although warm, the refreshing showers which continue to cool the air until about the 10th of May, and the almost never absent Westerly breezes, invited me daily to pass much of my leisure time in walking about the rock, to visit the numerous very interesting curiosities it contains. Following up this practice, Captain Evatt and myself very frequently sallied forth together, without any previously arranged design. Thus on the 21st of March we strolled out to the South, and on reaching a spot called Bonavista, we observed several ships endeavouring to get under-way, although there was at that moment scarcely a breath of wind. As usual, we took out our long telescopes, and resting them on the parapet wall, we followed the various operations of those ships.

We soon noticed the Minorca, at that time I think commanded by Captain Duncan, begin to move, but the wind was so light that she was nearly ungovernable; through this cause she drifted against a frigate lying at anchor, and carried away her own fore-top-sail-yard. The crash produced by the fracture was so loud, and the atmosphere so still, that although distant more than a mile, we heard it most distinctly.

The Prevoyante store ship took her departure at the same time towards the West, probably for England.

Very soon after this, about the 24th of March, Admiral Sir Sidney Smith arrived from England in the Pompey, of eighty guns, on his way to Palermo, and thence to join Admiral Sir I. T. Duckworth. Lieutenant Mercer, of the Royal Engineers, having arrived in the Pompey, was quartered in an old condemned building opposite to my house in South Port.

On the 29th of March I was invited by General Fox to meet Sir Sidney at dinner. I never was more amused or more delighted; Sir Sidney's details and spirited descriptions of several of his very intrepid achievements were highly interesting. After dinner, whilst taking coffee, I had a long conversation with Sir Sidney, who mentioned the practicability of throwing small shells by rockets to the distance of two thousand to two thousand five hundred yards; and I think he said he had succeeded in doing so. Be this as it may, my late very worthy friend, Sir William Congreve, some years afterwards put this mode of throwing five-and-a-half inch shells with great precision, into full and very effective practice.

I availed myself of this opportunity to remind Sir Sidney of a visit he had paid to the Warren at Woolwich, now called the Royal Arsenal, in 1793 or 1794, and that I had been present at some experiment, or something of that kind, which had induced him to attend on that occasion; and although he could not remember my person, as I was much too young to attract his notice, he immediately recollected the event, and gave me a full account of the details, which have, however, now totally escaped my memory. Yet time can never efface the deep impression he himself made on my mind, by his display of the best manner of using a dirk or dagger, one of which he wore at the time; and, I believe, that it was at about this period that dirks began to be used by the navy on common occasions instead of swords.

Several of the officers of the Artillery and Engineers then present at Woolwich, having expressed a desire that Sir Sidney should show them the manner of using the dirk to which he had alluded, he very kindly drew the one he had on, and with surprising agility and skill went through the exercise of defence and attack, supposing his adversary to be armed with a cutlass.

His attitude was with his right foot advanced, his body bent back, and his right arm raised and covering his forehead, holding the dagger or dirk, which had a strong and broad blade, pointed at his antagonist in a position to stab. "Then," said he, "should my opponent cut down at my head, I should drop the blade of the dirk along my arm, which it should cover up to my elbow; and in that position, by a very slight movement, I could guard to the left or right, receiving any cut on the blade of the dirk; then instantly, before my adversary could recover so as to make a second cut, I should plunge the dagger into him."

Thus Sir Sidney went through all the manœuvres for parrying every cut; and I must admit that I was greatly seduced by this display of the dirk *versus* cutlass. Sir Sidney Smith's figure, his activity, the brilliancy of his eye, and his black whiskers descending to the bottom of his throat, in those days never before seen, gave him an air of ferocity surpassing any Algerine and any Arab of the desert, which drew forth from every spectator the most unequivocal expressions of admiration.

I well remember that, just before this event, the summit of perfection in the way of sidearms amongst the officers was a fine, long, and well-curved hanger; and those officers who occasionally returned from the army, then serving in Holland and the Netherlands, under His Royal Highness the Duke of York, who could procure and bring over with them a regular French Carmagnole, were viewed with envy, and excited in the beholders the greatest ambition to be in possession of such an inestimable treasure, for which they might, and in some instances actually did, obtain very ridiculous prices; but now the ocular demonstration Sir Sidney had so obligingly given us of the infallibility of the dirk, had not only lowered the value of the Carmagnole to a discount, but, during many weeks and months afterwards, Sir Sidney, by management of the dirk, had left such an impression on the minds of all present, and had taken such powerful possession of the opinions of the young officers and cadets at Woolwich, that little else was talked of or thought of, and no weapon was regarded in any way as comparable with the dirk.

During the month of April (1806), we got up some very good races along the Western beach, within the Spanish Lines, particularly on the 19th, 23rd, and 28th, when Mrs. Short, the lady of an officer in the 10th Regiment of Foot, and Captain Francis Smith of the Royal Artillery, rode an excellent race; the lady won by a length. Lieutenant Mulcaster of the Royal Engineers, and Captain Ash of the 48th Regiment, also rode, when the latter won.

The concourse of Spanish officers and ladies, and others, attracted by the announcement of these races, was immense; many of them coming from Cadiz, Sevilla, Malaga, Ronda, and surrounding country. Those who had never before been present at an English race, were overwhelmed with astonishment at the speed of our horses, and at the manner of riding.

At this period, as there were several distinguished personages at Gibraltar, some going up the Mediterranean, whilst others were on their way to England, Mrs. Fyers, our Commandant's lady, invited many of them to dinner, and a much larger number to join in the evening, and form a full-sized soirée. I had staying with me a young connection of mine—a midshipman—who had served his time, and a few years to spare. The last ship he had belonged to was the Victory, and he had been the Signal Midshipman on the memorable event of the Battle of Trafalgar, when, as the Victory was going into action, Lord Nelson said, addressing him and several others who had in like manner served their time, "Now, you young dogs! you are always teazing me to get you made! This day you will be all made!" Nelson fell, and Spencer still remained a midshipman.

At the time I am noticing, Spencer was on his way to England, a passenger in the wardroom with some of his old mess-mates more fortunate than himself, on board the Dreadnought; and in which ship Admiral the Earl of Northesk was also going home a passenger. Mrs. Fyers had been so obliging as to send me an invitation to join the evening party; and although Spencer had not been included, I took the liberty of taking him with me. Mrs. Fyers soon introduced me to Lord

Northesk, and I seized the first opportunity for leading Spencer up to his lordship, and briefly acquainted him with the facts above mentioned, adding, that "I should esteem it as a favour done to myself, if, on arriving at Spithead, his lordship would give him a few lines to the Admiralty, and start him off, for we all know what wild dogs those boys are when they step on shore after a long absence." His lordship bowed most graciously several times, gave me a hearty shake of the hand, and promised to comply with my request. Before the anchor was down Spencer had received the letter, and an order to be off instanter. He passed his examination, and was made within a month after he arrived in England. So much for impudence! The Dreadnought sailed from Gibraltar on the 28th of April, 1806.

CHAPTER IV.

Parties and Excursions—Catland Bay—Pelted by the Monkeys—Party to St. George's Hall—Magnificent Scenery—Narrow escape from an immense stone hurled at us by the Monkeys—Ride about with General Fox—The Devil's Bowling-Green—Military Garden—Sir Joseph Banks and the Gloucestershire Prophet.

THE pic-nic parties commenced about this time, as also country excursions. Many of these were now formed for visiting Algeziras, San-Roque, the Castle of Andalucia, the Orange Grove, Ronda, and even as far as Tangiers, Tetuan, and Morocco. But to go to most of these places, a special permission was required, not only from the Governor, but the application to be sent to Algeziras as regarded all places in Spain, to receive the Spanish confirmation there, and be returned. All this evidently required a couple of days at least.

Notwithstanding this sort of obstruction, the applications were very numerous, and large parties thus almost daily filled the Spanish hotels, particularly the one at San-Roque.

However, as we were very frequently in a humour to enjoy little parties at a less distance, less expense, and at a shorter notice; we had recourse to a most charmingly secluded spot on the Eastern side of the Rock, called Catland Bay, of which the name is sufficient to bring to my recollection, in the liveliest colours, numberless parties of pleasure in that charming retreat. Such, indeed, were the attractions of its romantic scenery, and the delightful coolness of the shade, caused by the sun passing, at about one o'clock daily, behind the Rock which here formed the Western boundary of this place, and which rises perpendicularly to the height of about fourteen hundred feet, that, during nearly a whole summer, our mess assembled every Thursday at Catland Bay, there to dine under the thick foliage of grape-vines, trained so as to cover a large space by the side of a luxuriant vegetable garden, having a good well of fresh water within fifty yards of the sea.

During the preparations of cooking and spreading the tables, we usually passed an hour or two in rambling along the beach to the Southward, as far as the perpendicular cliff, which rises out of deep water to a vast height, and beyond which no one can advance on the shore. Others amused themselves in ascending the enormous bank of sand, extending from near the water's edge, at an angle of more than thirty degrees, to within three hundred or four hundred feet of the top of the rock, and consequently must be full one thousand feet high.

On these occasions we were frequently pelted by the monkeys; and one day, when I had nearly reached the top of this mountain of sand, my attention was drawn towards the impracticable cliff above, by the loud chattering and half-screaming voices of a multitude of monkeys. On looking up, I quickly perceived thirty to forty of them, leaping from edge to ledge, on the face of this frightful precipice, apparently almost perpendicular, with surprising accuracy, and, seemingly, totally divested of fear, until the greater portion of them had collected about one place, full two hundred feet up the cliff, and which was nearly abreast of the spot where I was labouring half-leg deep in the loose sand, to reach the summit.

Having with me my pocket spy-glass, I very soon discovered that they were engaged in endeavouring to push off, from a small recess, a large stone, weighing one hundred pounds at least.

It was very interesting to observe that, whilst some of them were pulling with their hands, others having taken up their position between the stone and the cliff, were kicking at it,—or rather with their feet against the stone, and their hands against the cliff, were jerking to throw it off.

These indefatigable creatures obstinately persevered in their efforts during seven or eight minutes; and although I could not discover that their exertions were simultaneous or united, at the end of that time they succeeded in hurling down the stone, which, after bounding twice or thrice in its descent from the most prominent portions of the cliff,—perhaps fortunately for me, buried itself firmly in the sand, instead of rolling down towards me— and so on to the sea, as I had expected.

On a previous occasion to the one just mentioned (the 22d March, 1806), a party having been formed on the preceding evening, for visiting St. George's Hall, amongst whom were Captain and Mrs. Fraser, of the 42d regiment, Captain and Mrs. Evatt, of the Royal Engineers, and myself, we set out at about ten o'clock, a servant being sent forward with refreshments.

Although the walk to the Hall is in some degree laborious, since it is situated about seven hundred feet higher than the town; yet, as the steepest part of the way may be ascended, through galleries cut out of the solid rock, and along deep open trenches, commencing at the Moorish Castle, we followed that road, and were thus greatly relieved from the heat of the sun, which, even at the date referred to above, begins to be very inconvenient.

In proceeding, we rested as often as we found it agreeable, and particularly at those places where we could admire the extensive and interesting views, stretching from Tangier and Cabrita Point, in the Straits of Gibraltar, nearly to Malaga, in the East, comprising the town of Algeziras, and the gigantic mountainous country in its rear; then, near the centre, we had a clear view of San Roque, and the lofty conical mount, called the Queen of Spain's Chair, with the rising mountains towards Ronda and Medina Sidoña rising above each other; and following on to our right, we perceive a bay, containing the small town of Estepona, whence the coast is distinctly seen in detail as far as Malaga. Behind Estepona, and extending past Malaga, but at a much greater distance, the snow-covered mountains of Granada are seen rising to a considerable height. The surface between the objects mentioned and the base of the Rock below, includes the Bay and part of the town of Gibraltar, the Neutral Ground, and fortifications of the Land-front, Old Mole, the Moorish Castle, &c., all of them seen nearly in plan.

During one of these halts, I observed on the face of the cliff, at no great distance from the spot where we were, a number of splendid squills in full bloom, as also some very fine everlasting flowers; upon which I made up my mind that on our return I would endeávour to get at some of them, and fill our basket, which then would be empty, with some of those rarities, as I then viewed them. We advanced very lazily, and after feasting on the grand prospect from the top of St. George's Hall, returned greatly delighted with our morning's walk to the spot where I had noticed the squills.

On examining the locality, I found it necessary to climb a steep, and somewhat dangerous part of the cliff, but which I accomplished without accident, and succeeded in procuring some very interesting plants.

The wind was sufficiently strong from the Eastward to drive the monkeys to the Northern cliffs; and as I had filled the basket, which rendered it heavy, Captain Fraser and myself were carrying it betwixt us, suspended on a stick, and were descending one of the open trenches, or lines of communication, when we suddenly heard the chattering of a great number of monkeys, at a few hundreds of feet above the spot we were passing, and in a moment afterwards, a stone weighing from fifteen to twenty pounds came down, bounding along with great force, and grazing the edge of my hat, fell betwixt Captain Fraser and myself. As Mrs. Evatt and Mrs. Fraser were following close behind with Captain Evatt, they saw the stone falling as it threatened our lives, and, as may be supposed, were greatly alarmed. However, after a short delay to recover the ladies, we thought it most prudent to hasten forward, lest we might not escape a second time so well.

Soon after my arrival at Gibraltar, I became a frequent visitor at the Convent, and I there passed many exceedingly pleasant evenings with the honourable General and Mrs. Fox, their two daughters, and Mr. Henry Fox, an only son, then about fourteen years of age, and also the Reverend Mr. Neave, his tutor, a gentleman eminently qualified for that important trust.

I believe that I was rather a favourite with the General, for whenever we met riding, he would either stop and exchange a few words, or sometimes invited me to accompany him; and he often listened with attention to my descriptions and details of various designs and projects for the improvements of the defences, the augmentation of cultivated ground, or the formation of additional roads, one especially to extend that leading to and terminating at the cottage appropriated to the summer residence of the Governor, and which I was anxious to have carried on by excavating it out of the solid rock until it should connect itself with the defences on the Northern face about Green's Lodge. I also had formed some very grand projects of improvements at the cottage,—pieces of water, fountains, shrubberies, &c., all of which had much amused the ladies of his family at various times when I walked with them over the grounds in the vicinity of the little villa.

On riding with the General towards Windmill Hill, one day, I pointed out the Devil's Bowling Green as a place which might in the course of time be cultivated as a military garden, although at that period it consisted of the roughest surface of solid rock, completely honey-combed to the depth of five to ten feet, yet the points of the rocks were all nearly of a uniform height. The General laughed at my scheme, and asked how I would proceed in order to fill up the cavities and deep holes, for there were no detached pieces, all was solid rock, so denuded of any kind of earthy particles that not a weed or even a palmetto bush could be traced on any part of it. The General grinned and smiled alternately, showing a sound set of teeth, which had, when a young man, been, no doubt, very handsome: but when I assured him I could accomplish that improvement very quickly, he said, "Well, but how should you perform it?" "I should encamp on those rocks the first Irish regiment that came to this garrison, and would supply three or four sledge-hammers to each tent, and at the same time I should prohibit the breaking or injuring of the rocks, but carefully avoid observing the infringement of my orders. Your excellency may depend upon it, that in less than a month, instead of the present rough Devil's Bowling Green, we should find it to be as level as the bowling-greens of the favourite tea-gardens in the vicinity of London."

" Very good !" exclaimed his excellency, and laughed most heartily.

"After this," I continued, " let all the scavengers' collections be brought here and spread over the broken rocks to the thickness of two or three feet; and in the space of a few months there will be the commencement of a most useful and very valuable vegetable garden ; and in the course of years the depth of earth will be fit for the growth of all those plants requiring abundance of rich soil. This mode of disposing of the sweepings of the streets would be far more proper than carrying them to the Neutral Ground, and there forming a meadow for the use of the Governor, and which is daily extending. This practice is highly objectionable in a military point of view, since it provides the besieging enemy with abundance of excellent materials for erecting the works of attack, instead of leaving him to make the most of the dry sand, which is probably the worst, excepting solid rock." The General again laughed in his usual subdued way at my explanation of the mode of executing this project, and said:

"Well, I really believe you would accomplish this scheme with little expense and great profit to the Government."

In this way I passed several very agreeable mornings, riding with the General until his usual dinner-hour, when on reaching his residence, he often invited me to dine with him. It was on one of these occasions, when the General and myself were passing along the side of his meadow on the Neutral Ground, on our way to the Eastern beach, or perhaps to Catland Bay, that we came upon a dozen or two of his sheep feeding there, accompanied by a black ram. His excellency, turning to me, said, "Are you acquainted with the celebrated Sir Joseph Banks?"

"Not particularly," was my reply. "I have been introduced to him by my father on his coming to Woolwich to see him, and

I have dined with him at his house in Soho Square."

"This great naturalist," observed the General, " who had circumnavigated the world with the well-known Captain Cook, had, amongst his numerous pursuits, turned his mind and attention to the study of meteorology, and heard that a man, by no means a scientific personage, who lived in comparative obscurity, was vastly clever, and never failed in his prophecies as regarded the prospects of the weather. On hearing of this man's peculiar talents, Banks could not fail to be inspired with a strong desire to converse with him, and judge for himself how far he had justly deserved the reputation he had acquired. At length a favourable opportunity presented itself for visiting the county of Gloucester, where this living barometer was located; and he hastened to profit by it for gratifying his desire. An interview was soon obtained, when Sir Joseph, after some satisfactory evidence of this man's extraordinary talent, inquired if he would instruct him in his cunning art. As he might have expected, the prophet declared in plain terms he would not, adding, 'I am consulted by persons residing both far and near, and I make a good living of it. You cannot, therefore, expect I should tell you how to take the bread out of my mouth.'

" 'Certainly not,' replied the President of the Royal Society; 'but for a sum of money you would not object.'

" 'Well,' our Gloucester friend replied, 'perhaps not.'

" Sir Joseph, fretting under the delay, at once said, 'Will one hundred pounds satisfy you?'

" 'I think, it would,' said the prophet, and the money was instantly put down.

" 'Now,' said the weather-wise Gloucestershire man, beckoning Banks to accompany him; and having scrambled up to the top of a high moor, tenanted by sheep only, he said to the President of the Royal Society, 'Do you see that black ram yonder?'

" 'Yes,' Banks replied.

" 'Well, then, whenever he turns his tail towards the South-west point of the compass, you may make sure rain is at hand!' "

CHAPTER V.

I request to be employed on actual service—Press General Fox to take me to Sicily with him—Edward Ellers, of the Navy—Sharp repartee, and loss of the Arrow—Take leave of Ellers—Kick up a row with the dogs—All's well—Kilvington—Alarm the fleet.— General Fox and family sail away to Messina.

ALTHOUGH I occupied a comfortable house, had an agreeable circle of acquaintance, and abundance of amusements, yet my anxiety to be employed on actual service was in no degree abated; and I had resolved on persevering in pressing my services to be engaged on any opportunity that might present itself.

The accounts of movements of troops at home, towards the sea-coast, preparatory to their embarcation on expeditionary service, which filled the daily newspapers; the accounts of our troops and armies in the field, invariably wounded my feelings, and seemed to reproach me for submitting to such a state of inactivity; and I constantly felt as if it were my own fault that I still remained on garrison duty.

This ambition being constantly uppermost, and having occasion to address a letter to Lieutenant-Colonel Rowley, at this time either Major-of-Brigade or Deputy-Inspector-General of Fortifications, on the 7th of March, 1806, I concluded that letter with the following expression of my views. " I look forward with great confidence to your not allowing any opportunity to escape for employing me on field service, and that you will respectfully remind the General (Morse) of my application to that effect in September last." But to this letter I never received any reply.

On the 30th of May, Brigadier-General the Honourable Robert Meade, under whom I had served at Gosport, arrived in the bay from England, with the 21st, 27th, 31st, and 35th

Regiments, on their way to Sicily, which gave rise to various rumours as to the object of this additional force; and amongst others, it was said to be destined to proceed to Egypt. This event gave a fresh stimulus to my desire to be so employed; and as shortly afterwards it was currently asserted that General Fox was to proceed to Sicily and assume the chief command of the expedition, I thought this a most favourable opportunity for renewing my efforts to be employed on active service.

I therefore, on the 16th of June, addressed a very pressing letter to his Excellency, soliciting to have the honour of being employed in the army destined to proceed under his command.

On the second day I received a very kind note from the General, written by himself, and expressing his regret at being unable to comply with my request in consequence of his having so repeatedly and so pressingly urged the necessity of employing two Captains of Engineers at Gibraltar; he, therefore, could not now immediately, after this recommendation had been complied with, disturb that arrangement by taking me away.

I was very deeply mortified at this failure; for, independently of my desire to be attached to any of our armies serving in the field, I had contracted a very sincere personal regard and attachment for the General and his amiable family.

Just at this period, early in the month of May, my old friend, Lieutenant Edward Ellers, of the Royal Navy, arrived at Gibraltar, in the Orion, Captain Codrington; and at the departure of that ship to join the fleet blockading the harbour of Cadiz, on the 18th of the same month, 1806; Ellers, at that time being in bad health, was invalided, as it is termed in the navy, and sent on shore to the navy hospital. In consequence of this event, Ellers passed much of his time with me; and on one occasion, having some days before accidentally heard of the brilliant action fought by Captain Vincent, commanding the Arrow, in which ship Ellers was at the time serving as second Lieutenant, but which he had not even hinted at, I requested him to relate to me the details of that desperate exploit. Ellers complied, and related the action then

recently fought by the Arrow, Captain Vincent, and the Acheron, bomb ketch, Captain Farquar, on the 5th of February, 1805 ; and a very faithful account of the same I find recorded in Marshall's Royal Naval Biography, under the head of the services of Richard Budd Vincent, Esq. But my worthy and modest friend, Ellers, omitted every mention of his own deeds, nor did he record a sharp repartee by one of the sailors of the Arrow, which the gallant First Lieutenant, since then Admiral Daly, obligingly communicated to me some forty-two years afterwards, one morning at the Senior United Service Club, as follows :—
" When the Arrow was actually sinking, in consequence of the severe damage she had sustained from the fire of the Incorruptible and Hortence, French frigates, off Algiers, Lieutenant Ellers and several of the seamen jumped over-board to save themselves from going down with the ship, and they were fortunately picked up by the Incorruptible's boats, which, at the same time, rescued the crew of the sinking ship from going down also ; and it was on this occasion that one of

the French Lieutenants employed in the boats, in a coarse, insulting manner, pompously declared, in tolerably good English, 'You proud English! we shall sweep the seas of you yet;' upon which he was promptly answered by one of the common seamen, an Irishman, named Casey, 'That may be; but, by Jazes! you have not yet got the broom that will do that.'"

Ellers had been about a month at the hospital, when I learnt the Orion had just returned into the bay, on purpose to carry General Fox, family and suite, to Sicily. I was anxious to announce this event to Ellers, as he was sufficiently recovered to re-embark, and I knew it would be very agreeable to him.

Accordingly, on the evening of the 21st of June, 1806, I availed myself of the cool, refreshing breeze, and accompanied by Captain Kilvington, of the Royal Engineers, I walked out to the hospital, where I had much pleasure in receiving Doctor Bell's confirmation that Ellers had fully recovered his health, and might join the Orion on the following day. Ellers was delighted at the prospect of having the General and the ladies of his family, and some of the staff, as passengers; and we passed the evening very pleasantly. Ellers having given us some cold beef and pickles, and a glass of negus, the usual bachelor's supper at Gibraltar in those days, Kilvington and myself shook hands with Ellers and the doctors, and took our departure towards town, at about half-past ten o'clock; but instead of following the most direct road, the night being delightfully refreshing, and the stars seeming to be brighter and more numerous than usual, we descended by a very steep road, called Tumble-Down-Dick, to near the New-Mole, thence by the ramparts along the saluting battery, &c., extending from near the New-Mole to Ragged-Staff. Close under this portion of the Lime-Wall, lay the prizes or vessels captured from the enemy, until condemned and finally disposed of. The shore being here tolerably steep, these vessels were generally ranged with their bows towards the land, packed side by side, touching each other; and they were so numerous, that they occupied a considerable length of the beach.

We occasionally stopped, and resting our

elbows on the parapet, lazily contemplated the tranquillity of the scene before us; and the total absence of any sound, invited us to converse on the monotonous life which the keepers or watchmen on board of those prizes must be doomed to lead.

At times, I thought I heard the splashing of oars in the offing, and yet, although both of us listened with particular attention, we, nevertheless, remained in doubt as to the fact; upon which I said it might be some boats passing from one ship-of-war to another, for these always occupied the outside of the anchorage; yet the sound appeared to be at a much greater distance. Kilvington hereon observed, that it might be Spanish boats, coming over from Algeziras, to endeavour to cut out some of our vessels, which at times lay in the bay too far from the batteries and men-of-war, to be well protected; and, although these attempts were very bold and hazardous, they had more than once been attended with success. "Not in such calm weather," thought I. "But," continued Kilvington, "since then, a large watch-dog has been kept on board each of the prizes, which has been found an excellent protection, not only against the Spanish boats, but also to prevent nocturnal plundering and pilfering, which, until then, had been practised to a serious amount."

Nothing further disturbed the stillness of the night, excepting, at intervals, a few unconnected chords struck on a guitar, which seemed to come from the direction of Guasco's garden, and resembled the floating notes of an Æolian harp. But these had ceased during some minutes, when we heard the periodical " All's well !" called out by every sentinel on the rock, in regular succession, as prescribed by garrison orders; and, as many of these sentinels were advantageously situated for producing echoes, the " All's well !" so often repeated in every variety of voice, was caught up by innumerable cliffs, and thrown back, " *well—well—well,*" until totally extinct; whilst in the North, as the calls came from the sentinels in the lines and elevated Moorish castle, and from the batteries still higher, they were so faint, yet so beautifully clear, that they seemed to descend from the regions above.

Whilst this line of calls rapidly faded away, in ascending to the elevated fortifications at Willis's, Green's Lodge, &c., another chain came floating towards us, by the Line-Wall, growing louder and louder, and then quickly passing on; around the South to Windmill Hill and Europa Point, the voices of the sentinels grew so faint as to leave it uncertain, when the last "All's well!" had been proclaimed.

The solemn and very imposing effect thus produced on my mind, actually fascinated me to the spot,—I felt what I could not describe; when Kilvington turned to me and said:— "That 'All's well!' has almost brought tears into my eyes, and yet, for the life of me, I cannot tell why." " I, also, have experienced a sensation of a very peculiar description, and, like yourself, am quite unable to reason upon the cause."

Having remained absorbed in silent and romantic meditation for some time, Kilvington observed it was late, and proposed that we should think of home; but, just as we were moving off, I heard one of the watch-dogs in the prizes make a noise which somewhat exceeded a growl, without amounting to a bark, but participated of both, and which induced me, without any definite object, to imitate the barking of a large dog; this challenge had no sooner reached the dogs, than it was answered by one or two of those trustworthy sentinels. I soon repeated the menace, to which I received a louder reply from a dozen at least, pronounced with extraordinary vigour, and in a tone nearly reaching to the highest pitch of their voices. Other dogs now added the strongest and boldest expressions of their sentiments, in a very unequivocal manner; and, from that moment, a violent and most animated contest was established amongst the whole of them.

The effect was truly amusing to us; and it was worthy of remark, that the same cliffs which but a while before had, with so much zeal and fidelity, cried out "All's well," were now actively engaged in multiplying the sounds of alarm and discord.

After diverting ourselves in this boyish way during a full quarter of an hour, we proceeded towards home, much delighted with our having kicked up such a row amongst the prizes; but the dogs went on barking at one another, and at the echoes of their voices, until, no doubt, they were quite exhausted.

On the following morning, a Lieutenant and a Midshipman of the Navy came in to breakfast with me, but I cannot now remember their names. They said they were as hungry as sharks, for they had been rowing guard all night; upon which I observed I had not heard that such a duty was customary in the bay. "Oh, as to customary, that is not a regular duty. But last night the rascally Spaniards came across the bay from Algeziras, to cut out some of the prizes, and they, no doubt, would have succeeded, had it not been for the famous watch-dog which every one of them has on board. On hearing this, we dropped our boats into the water and gave chase; but although, at times, we could see them quite distinctly, such was the art and cunning of these fellows, or, perhaps, they were favoured by streams of mist or fog, floating across our course, in an instant between them and us, that we occasionally lost sight of them; and so it went on, till we chased them in right under the guns of Pigeon Island" (at Algeziras).

With the gravest face I could put on, I inquired at what hour this desperate attempt had been made; when they replied that it was at about eleven o'clock, or soon after.

These lads were by far too much exalted at the important service they had rendered their country, to allow of any disclosure of the fact; and, moreover, I was not on terms so intimate with them, as to induce me to let them into a little bit of a secret, as to who the real enemy was, and which might have caused me a great deal of unpleasantness; so, all things being well considered, I thought it most prudent to join them in abusing the rascally privateers.

Kilvington now came in, full of our last night's adventure, and was beginning to relate the affair, when I called him to leave the room with me, under pretext of having something of the utmost importance to communicate; but his desire to tell the story was so strong, that I found it no easy matter to get him out in time.

During several days after this affair, I was greatly diverted at the variety of versions related of this ridiculous event; the minutest details and fullest particulars were carried about with astonishing zeal.

On the 27th of June, with unfeigned regret I followed Mrs. Fox, and all the family, excepting the General, to Ragged Staff, and having seen them safely embarked on board of the Orion, I returned home, taking Ellers with me, and passed a rather dull evening. On the following morning, at nine o'clock, I attended the General, and embarked with him, amidst salutes from the battery and ship, each firing nineteen guns; and as the Orion was quite ready to proceed, in less than a quarter of an hour she was under way.

The names of the officers on the Staff of his Excellency, and who embarked with him, were:—Major Mohr, of De Roll's, and Captain Young, of the 10th Foot, aides-de-camp; Lieutenant-Colonel Ainy, Military Secretary.

At parting, the General gave me a hearty

shake of the hand, and repeated his regret at being unable to comply with my request; and in like manner I received from the whole of the family very kind expressions. I have never seen any of the party since that day.

CHAPTER VI.

General Drummond assumes the command—Excursions —War on the water and peace on land—General Castaños—Lieutenant Blaquier, R.N.—Amateur Theatricals—Pizarro—Doctor O'Rorke takes his leave of the stage.

GENERAL DRUMMOND now assumed the chief command, and from him and his family I experienced very marked civility.

Time now glided on very agreeably; for, although Gibraltar, during time of war with Spain, has been commonly described as a sort of small island on a ship, in consequence of the very limited extent of its surface, yet the mornings might be profitably passed at the splendid garrison library reading-room, or in riding into Spain ; and the constant succession of evening parties, balls given by the Governor, and those supported by subscription at the library, provided a sufficient round of amusements, to render the days passed at Gibraltar frequently the subject of pleasing recollections. Moreover, notwithstanding our being at war with Spain, the most friendly intercourse was maintained, with this very strange anomaly,—that whilst we frequently visited the towns of San Roque, Algeziras, Ronda, and even sometimes leave might be obtained to go to Malaga and Cadiz, to the latter with an American passport; yet, on the water, our hostility was in full vigour.

Of this very extraordinary description of warfare I could relate endless illustrative anecdotes; yet, one or two, which passed immediately under my own eyes, and in which I was interested, may be deemed sufficient, and of which the following are faithful narrations;—but I must step back a few days:—

On the 17th June, 1806, when General Fox was about to embark for Sicily, the Spanish General Castaños, Captain-General of the province of Andalucia, came from Algeziras to Gibraltar, on purpose to pass the day with the General, and take leave of him on his departure from the Rock. I was on this occasion invited to dine at the Convent, and during the evening I had frequent opportunities of conversing in the French language with General Castaños, who appeared to entertain a very friendly disposition towards me, and amongst many questions inquired if I had as yet visited Algeziras, to which I replied that I had not; he then said, "I shall be very glad to see you whenever it may be agreeable and convenient to you, and I hope you will not long deprive me of this pleasure."

On the following day I received from the General a permanent pass, ordering the Spanish authorities to allow me to disembark at Algeziras from any boat without obstruction, and to proceed whithersoever I might please to go, —a degree of accommodation, and a mark of politeness, which he had not before this time granted to any individual. And in the note accompanying the pass, he expressed a wish that I should use it frequently, and that the only condition he should impose on me was, that I should invariably dine with him on these occasions, and introduce any of my friends I should think proper to take with me to Algeziras. The above statement sufficiently shows how we carried on the war on shore, and the following anecdote will mark the feelings of the same people when floating on the water.

We had, during the war with Spain, several gun-boats in constant readiness to assist and protect our shipping, as often as required, against the attacks made by the Spanish privateers and gun-boats stationed at Algeziras; and a Lieutenant Blaquier, of the Royal Navy, was during a long period one of the officers employed on this important and valuable service. Opportunities for performing gallant exploits were not wanting, and Blaquier never allowed one to escape him. He thus frequently distinguished himself in a very conspicuous manner by the intrepid and effectual protection which he almost daily afforded to our merchant ships, and to the vessels employed in the transport of live stock from the coast of Africa to Gibraltar.

One morning I sallied forth to the Neutral Ground to take an agreeable walk along the Western sea beach, when I was attracted by the cooling breeze to extend my ramble beyond the Spanish Lines; and which, strange as it may appear, required no other passport than a civil word and a cigar to the sentinel, who, with the utmost courtesy, would reply, "*passa-um adelante*,"—please to go forward; and so on I went, till I arrived at a Spanish battery, which we denominated the Black Battery.

At the entrance I was met by a Spanish officer of artillery, with whom I happened to be acquainted, for he had several times before this dined at our mess, and he invited me into his guard-room. Having exchanged a few ordinary compliments, he accepted a cigar, and provided a bottle of Catalonian wine, which, mixed with a large quantity of water, I found exceedingly refreshing.

For some time before this I had heard a slight cannonading in the Bay, but this was an event of such constant occurrence, that I had taken no notice of it. This firing had ceased, when a serjeant entered, and reported to his officer that an English gun-boat, although struggling with every effort of her crew to make good her retreat into Gibraltar, was drifting by the strength of the tide and wind directly towards the battery we were in, and that he believed the boat was then within range. The officer ordered the guns to be instantly manned and prepared for action, and he himself went out to ascertain the accuracy of the serjeant's statement.

In a few moments my friend returned, and with the utmost politeness made me a low bow, and smilingly said, " I deeply regret that I am under the unpleasant necessity of requesting you will do me the favour to withdraw from the battery, as I am about to fire on one of your gun-boats, and etiquette requires that I should not allow you, whom I must *pro formá* regard as an enemy, to remain within the battery during the firing. You need not," added he, " absent yourself further than a few yards, for as soon as I shall have sunk that boat, we may as well finish our bottle, and I shall have much pleasure in smoking another of your exquisite havannahs."

Having complied with the etiquette, as he termed it, I took up a station about thirty yards to the left of the battery, whence, with the aid of my three-foot telescope, (my constant companion when rambling out of town or up the mountain,) I could distinctly recognise Lieutenant Blaquier dressed in a pair of white trowsers, and standing on the boom, steadying himself at the same time by one of the ropes which he held in his hand.

Several shots were soon fired at him, and by their ranging much beyond the boat, the accuracy of the serjeant's report as to distance was fully established. My attention was momentarily diverted from my glass by a peasant who came up, and asked me some unimportant question; when two guns were fired nearly simultaneously, and in the next instant I heard a general shout from the soldiers in the battery. I must confess that I felt my blood run cold through my veins, and hastily directing my glass on the boat, in expectation of seeing her sinking, I examined her from stern to stern without being able to discover any damage or change, excepting that Blaquier, although still standing on the boom, was without his hat on his head; but I saw it almost immediately handed up to him by one of the sailors.

I afterwards discovered that Blaquier's hat had been accidentally knocked off by a rope, just as the shots were passing, which gave rise to the shout from the battery, the gunners believing that Blaquier's head had been carried off.

Having very soon discovered that he should not be able to make good his retreat against wind and tide, or rather the current, Blaquier pulled directly towards a Portuguese ship of war, which he succeeded in reaching; and holding on to her side, was thus relieved from the risk of being struck by shot from the Spanish battery, which could not keep up its fire whilst he remained in that position, as they might accidentally strike the Portuguese, which was a neutral ship, instead of the boat.

I was now invited to finish our bottle; and as soon as the tide had turned, Blaquier let go his hold of the Portuguese, and in five minutes was out of reach of the Spaniards, who, did not think the chance of hitting him sufficient to justify the expenditure of another discharge from the guns.

It was now very interesting to observe that the same man who for the last half-hour had been most zealously endeavouring to destroy Blaquier and his brave crew, was also the first to propose drinking to his health, adding, "I feel delighted at having most scrupulously discharged my duty towards my king, without, at the same time, having to condole with you on the loss of your gallant friend."

I was particularly pleased by this declaration; for, while it was expressive of his loyalty, and manifested his respect for, and the overwhelming importance he attached to, his military duty; yet, at the same time, it indicated a mind possessing noble moral feelings, totally divested of any personal animosity.

I now took an affectionate leave of this worthy officer, and hastened back to Gibraltar, having just recollected that our mess dinner had been ordered to be ready an hour earlier than usual, in consequence of a theatrical performance that evening by amateur officers of the garrison. These representations were invariably well and very fully attended; and the piece to be performed that evening was "Pizarro, or the Spaniards in Peru." Doctor O'Roarke, a very good-natured Irishman, but by no means qualified to acquire much theatrical celebrity, had so much pressed his services, that at length he was permitted to take the part of the blind man.

As I was on terms of intimate acquaintance with O'Roarke, I became interested in the due performance of his part; and I accordingly bestowed some time and pains in trying to perfect him in the very few words he would have to recite, and particularly in endeavouring to teach him how to pronounce those few words free from the brogue.

At six o'clock I accompanied O'Roarke to the theatre, and stuck to him up to the moment of his sallying forth, making him repeat after me a hundred times at least, "lead me, child," which he as often would pronounce, with his pure native accent, "lade may, childe."

At length, the curtain was drawn up with

due solemnity, when Elvira was discovered extended on a couch. Lieutenant Williams, of the Royal Engineers, a very excellent *amateur* performer, had undertaken the part of Elvira, for we had no actresses; and his figure was admirably well calculated to perform the female character, he being very short, fair, and without whiskers,—and moreover, his features were favourable.

Williams, on this occasion, either accidentally or waggishly, had so disposed his lower garment that Elvira exposed somewhat more of her leg than merely the ancle, yet it was but very little more. Upon the discovery of this, some of the audience expressed a considerable degree of displeasure, whilst others laughed heartily, and applauded. Williams took no notice of this little contest, but rose and advanced to the front of the stage, in order to proceed with the performance. Had this little event been here dropped, all would have gone on well enough, but a number of the younger officers occupying seats in the pit, imprudently, I had almost said impertinently, repeated, and kept up a sharp hissing, in which they could not have indulged had they reflected on the indecency of such conduct towards a company of amateur performers. Williams now, as might have been anticipated, felt the independence of his own position, whilst he was equally sensible of the reverse being exactly that of the audience; he, therefore, at once determined on letting them feel the consequence thereof. The lofty, majestic, and solemn air of Elvira was suddenly dropped, and replaced by a lively, skipping dance—partly jig and partly hornpipe,—which Williams kept up during a minute or two, whistling and snapping his fingers, and rocking his head from side to side with an air of angry defiance. Having then completed the circuit of the stage, Elvira waved her hand most gracefully and full of sentiment, and with infinite dignity of manner, and softness of voice, expressed the deepest regret at having given such mortal offence; and then retired, amidst the loudest applause and hisses.

Notwithstanding that great efforts were made by officers sent from the boxes with the most pressing entreaties of the ladies, Williams stoutly refused to go on again ; and the part of Elvira was unavoidably read.

This event, it will be readily understood, had somewhat disturbed that unanimous harmony so necessary on similar occasions. However, as the performance proceeded, the general excitement which had been so improperly raised, partly subsided; I persevered in my task with O'Roarke, and got him, as I thought, tolerably perfect by the time when it came to his turn to go forth, so that when called upon by the stage-manager, he stepped out boldly.

Unfortunately, however, friend O'Roarke, who wore spectacles, had neglected to take them off, which instantly caught the attention of the audience, upon which a burst of laughter sounded from every part of the pit ; this was, no doubt, rather disconcerting on a first appearance on the boards; yet, I think, O'Roarke might have stood his ground, although much disturbed, had he not by this time lost all the benefit of the instruction which I had so industriously bestowed on him, for in the next minute out came "*lade may, childe,*" with so much brogue, that a loud voice from the centre of the house called out, "Ough! look, my dear, at the Irishman in Peru;" upon which another retorted, "Ough! honney, that's nothing at-all, at-all, to a blind man with spectacles on." None could now resist joining in the laugh; and amidst shouts and cries of "Bravo, bravissimo!" "Anchor! anchor!" "Go off!" "Stay on!" "Come on!" "Pluck-up!" "Go it!" and a thousand similar expressions, rendered almost inaudible by the stamping of feet, clapping of hands, beating with sticks, &c.,—poor O'Roarke made but one bound off the stage, and so "took his leave of the show-folks;" for he had vanished to appear no more.

On these occasions we always had the pleasure of being treated with some very good songs, chiefly of the comic class; and none were more esteemed than those supplied by Mr. Gill, a Lieutenant and Adjutant in the 48th Regiment. Lieutenant Bruguier, of the Royal Navy, also contributed largely on these occasions. That gentleman was, not long after this period, unfortunately killed in a duel by an officer in the 48th Regiment.

CHAPTER VII.

The great powder-magazine in danger of blowing-up—
The Author had already saved another powder magazine from blowing-up at Quebec—Blue Peter—
Monkey caught in the act—Witness a bull-fight—
Narrow escape.

SOME time after this affair, having been invited to pass the evening at the house of one of my friends, at that time quartered in the South, at about eleven o'clock I took my departure homewards, my road leading me between the great powder-magazine near Rozier Bay, and some houses on the right, in one of which Mr. Pownall, the storekeeper, resided.

The sallies of wit which had enlivened the evening, and several most amusing songs with which some of the party had kindly entertained us, were still dancing in my thoughts as I approached the magazine; and I was at that moment endeavouring to revive the pleasure I had experienced on the first hearing of one of the comic songs by humming it over *sotto voce*, when my charming reveries were suddenly disturbed by a smell strongly resembling that of a burning slow match, and which, as may be expected, not only knocked the music out of my head, but filled me with intense anxiety. I, therefore, lost not one moment in proceeding to search after the cause of this alarming circumstance, by changing my position in the vicinity of the magazine, and by walking entirely round the outer wall; by this means I very soon ascertained that the smell increased as I approached the magazine.

Such a discovery, it will be readily imagined, raised in me the most serious and startling apprehensions, not only for my personal safety, but also for that of a large portion of the troops quartered in the South Barracks, and some hundreds of inhabitants in the neighbourhood.

Completely stupified for a moment, I remained motionless and irresolute. Self-preservation by flight was, as is usual on these occasions, the first course which suggested itself; but in an instant I felt that such an abandonment of hope, whilst any could be entertained, would be cowardly; I, therefore, resolved on immediately using every effort to avert a calamity so dreadful, that no one could have ventured to estimate its extent.

Much depended on acting with promptitude; any step was better than standing still. This had no sooner passed through my mind, than I at once ran off to Pownall's house, and fortunately found him at home. With as much caution as time could admit, I communicated my apprehension, and offered to accompany him to the magazine.

Pownall's countenance suffered no change; with a firm step and a degree of calmness I could not have anticipated, he seized upon the keys, lighted a lanthorn, and off we started across a small open space lying between his house and the magazine. We encountered a short obstruction from the sentinel, who being unacquainted with Pownall's person, would not, without my presence in uniform, have allowed him to approach the outer door in the enclosure wall. Just as Pownall introduced the key, a bright flash made us start backwards a couple of yards at least in breathless agitation, and whilst staring into each other's faces in the hope of receiving some explanation, another brighter flash satisfied us that it was merely distant lightning.

Pownall now returned to the door, and without allowing any time for being again diverted from our purpose, he turned the key, and threw open the door in a breath.

All appeared safe enough on entering; no light was discoverable; there was not even now any smell of the match. A light air was blowing across between us and the magazine-door, which we had scarcely noticed. Pownall went off to the left to walk round the building within the enclosure, and I proceeded to examine the portion on the right, when again the smell of the burning match suddenly increased as I reached a spot exactly to leeward of the magazine-door.

I now followed the stream of this scent, and was not long in finding my nose close up to the outer door of the magazine, the smell of the match increasing as I advanced. At this moment Pownall had just completed his walk round the building, and with much glee reported that all was right, for he had been unable to discover anything amiss, and that the smell of the match could not proceed from within the enclosure wall.

"You are all wrong if you think so," replied I, " bring your lanthorn here;" for by this time I fancied I could see some thin streams of smoke, as if issuing from a small aperture. Pownall accordingly came up, and we both distinctly saw the smoke in white curling threads creeping out from the keyhole.

Every doubt as to the position of the fire was now removed; it actually proceeded from within the magazine itself! and what hope could there be of extinguishing it before the explosion? or, might not the attempt to do so accelerate the fatal moment? I freely confess I regarded myself as a dead man, when I considered the chances of escape to be a thousand to one at least; ay, ten thousand to one against me.

In short, my feelings were those usually described as having the hair standing on end. Pownall boldly introduced the key, and unlocked the external door of the lobby, but suddenly paused, observing, he feared the admission of the slightest current of air;— "Fortunately," continued he, "there is no wind this night."

"We have now gone too far to hesitate or to retreat. We have but one course to follow. Let us do our duty, trusting in God to protect us."

Having thus expressed my feelings, I placed my hand on the key, which was still in the lock, and very carefully drew open the door. Oh! it was truly appalling! The volume of thick smoke, slightly tinged with red, was awful in the extreme, and almost deprived us of the power of respiration. In less than a quarter of a minute, the density of the smoke had sufficiently diminished to allow us to perceive the large red cinder of a slow match, the whole of which, including all the windings round the stick, had been burnt, and was reduced to a red cinder, still retaining its delicate hold of the stick, but ready to fall to pieces on the slightest agitation of the atmosphere. A portion also of the woodwork of the handle or stick was reduced to a red charcoal.

Our fears of doing anything that might agitate the minutest portion of the surrounding atmosphere was, no doubt, similar to that related of travellers in the Alps, who, when in certain situations, dare not speak to each other in a louder voice than a whisper, lest it should cause the fall of an avalanche.

Nothing could be more perplexing, yet, after a short reflection, I took off my hat, and having, with the greatest gentleness, put it under the burning cinder of the slow match, with equal care I took the match-stick near the bottom, and turned the whole upside down into the hat, covering up the same with my handkerchief, closed the sides of my folding cocked-hat as much together as I could, and thus completely confined the fire within the hat. Oh! no tongue can relate the degree of pride I felt, and the triumph with which I marched out to a large tub full of water, which Pownall pointed out, and into which I plunged the whole together. The most unbounded joy succeeded to a state of anxiety which I shall not attempt to describe.

Pownall and myself having congratulated each other on the happy issue of this alarming affair, parted, agreeing that although it was desirable not to give publicity to this negligence, still to prevent any future want of precaution, I should see General Smith, commanding the artillery, and acquaint him with the event. The General thanked me, and requested secrecy might be observed; yet the event got wind, but ended without much noise being made about it.

I afterwards ascertained that a salute had been fired from the saluting battery in the afternoon of that day; and no doubt could exist of the match having been imperfectly extinguished when put into the lobby of the magazine; a most improper place, and which from this moment was discontinued.

On my way home I could not help musing on the singularity of the fact, that I should have been twice concerned in extinguishing a fire greatly endangering the explosion of a powder magazine; for in the year 1799, when quartered at Quebec, the whole of the Engineers' work-shops were consumed by fire. These buildings were all lightly constructed of wood, and were situated near the gate of Saint Louis; the large stock of timber, deals, boards, &c., were also consumed. This event occurred during the severest part of the winter, at a time when the Fahrenheit thermometer was between twenty and thirty degrees below zero.

The drums beating to arms, and quick tolling of the church-bells, had speedily roused the garrison and spread the usual alarm amongst the inhabitants; when I hastily left my bed, and with accelerated speed found my way to the fire, by following the reflected glare of light in the sky.

On reaching the scene of action, as soon as I could find him, I reported my presence to Colonel Gother Mann, at that time the Commanding Royal Engineer in the Canadas, and

Commandant of the Garrison, at Quebec. I was not allowed to remain a very long time unemployed, and thus soon received orders to direct and superintend the removal of some stacks of timber to a secure distance from danger, and also to throw snow, with broad wooden shovels made for that purpose, upon such parts as had not yet caught fire.

In about an hour after my arrival on the ground, a strong wind began to blow exactly in the direction from the fire towards a powder-magazine, situated at no great distance.

This magazine was built of stone and arched over, I believe, with brick, but it was covered with shingles or thin pieces of wood similar to tiles or slates, fastened on rafters forming a roof to keep the wet from the arch. Large flakes of fire were now carried along with the wind, some of them much beyond the magazine, but others mischievously fell on the wooden roof, which in a short time was on fire in several places.

The general alarm which this event immediately occasioned can be very easily imagined; and whilst Colonel Mann ordered the whole of the troops (hitherto engaged in endeavouring to extinguish the flames with snow, and in cutting off the fire from extending) to retire from the scene of danger, and seek protection on the outside of the fortifications, by escaping out of the gate of Saint Louis, I was directed, with a Serjeant and twenty men, to advance to the magazine and extinguish the fire on the roof, which now began to burn furiously; but Colonel Mann gave me no detailed instructions of any description, leaving the manner of executing the order entirely to my own judgment.

I accordingly started with my men, and taking two ladders with me, of which there were many lying about the ground, I ran up to the magazine, encouraging the men by assuring them that it was impossible for the powder in the magazine to catch fire through such thick walls.

My first step was to order all the air-holes to be filled with snow; and then as I ascended the first ladder that was laid on the roof, I ordered the men to follow my example. I then made them take off their great coats (made of blanketing), and hand them up to me full of snow; directing the Serjeant to follow my example on the second ladder. My orders were obeyed with alacrity; the snow was passed up the ladders from hand to hand by the men standing closely packed on the same, in the same way as buckets of water are passed along. As I received a coat full, I emptied it before me, spreading it forward, and following it on my hands and knees, I went on covering the burning wood with more snow, until I had extinguished, with the aid of the Serjeant, the whole of the fire, and which at one time extended to about one sixth part of the roof.

Having completed this service, I marched back my party to the other buildings on fire, and I desired the Serjeant to employ this small force to the best of his judgment, whilst I went to report the successful result of my efforts.

In searching about for Colonel Mann, I fell in with the Commander-in-Chief, his Excellency Lieutenant-General Peter Hunter, to whom I reported the accomplishment of Colonel Mann's orders, and upon which his satisfaction was expressed thus:—" I say, young gentleman, you have not been long about it; I hope it is well done." No other notice of this event was taken, although several of the officers and corps were thanked in garrison and general orders. Colonel Mann was the Commandant of the garrison, and probably had thought that, as I was of his corps, any particular mention of me would have been regarded as an act of partiality. I was, nevertheless, a little disappointed.

His Excellency Lieutenant-General Peter Hunter was a man of singular habits—he chewed tobacco, drank rum and water instead of wine, and, in addressing any person, he invariably commenced with "I say." He wore shoes, and long black cloth tight-fitting gaiters up to the caps of his knees, and blue cloth breeches, whence he attracted upon himself the *sobriquet* of *Blue Peter;* he was blunt and coarse in his manners, and was never known to have been civil to any body.

One morning, in the course of my tour of inspection of the works of the North District, I was waiting in a shaded spot near Princess Charlotte's battery, which I was then constructing or rather chiselling out of the solid rock, the artificers being about to suspend their labours, in order to take their dinners: I noticed a little drummer come up to that elevated place, and, without delay, deposited a can, containing his father's dinner, in the usual place, some thirty yards away from the battery. His father gave him a nod, and away went the boy to barracks. At this time, the wind was blowing strong from the Eastward, which invariably drives away the monkeys from the back of the rock to the sheltered side above the town. They were very numerous on this occasion, and they had been amusing themselves in gamboling about, and seemed to be exceedingly merry, throwing stones down the steep declivity above us; but the arrival of the little drummer had attracted their notice, and his deposit of the can had not escaped their observation. As the can seemed to be somewhat unprotected, the cupidity or the curiosity of the monkeys was encouraged, and they began to creep on very stealthily towards its locality; and anxiously longing for an opportunity, which the departure of the little man in red uniform so much favoured, in a minute or two, monkey after monkey advanced a yard at a time, keeping a watchful eye, alternately bent on me and on the can, when, presently, the biggest and boldest darted at the prize, and, in the twinkling of an eye, the lid of the can was lifted, and the monkey inserted his head above his ears with some force; and then, but not until then, he discovered the error he had committed. One of my men started off to secure Mr. Joco, which the poor creature soon heard, when, darting off at all hazards, he fell, helplessly battering the can in all directions, without being able to extricate his head from the chancery into which he had so unguardedly placed it. Joco was at once secured, bound hands and feet, and carried away into perpetual slavery.

From the time when I arrived at Gibraltar, I began to anticipate that my long-existing desire to witness a bull-fight would at length be gratified. I was, therefore, very much delighted on being informed that a succession of exhibitions of that nature, which for some weeks had been the general subject of conversation, were now finally settled, and would commence in a few days. On the announcement of the first day's sport, almost every officer in the garrison made arrangements for attending at these horrid spectacles on some one of the days. Leave of absence was granted to a limited number of each regiment and corps, and some were permitted to pass the night at San-Roque.

Accordingly, on the 30th of August, 1806, Lieutenant Williams, of the Royal Engineers, and myself, went to San-Roque on the first day; and having taken dinner at an early hour, by four o'clock we repaired to a large amphitheatre, erected for the purpose with timber, and occupying the whole of the great square.

A spacious and decorated box was prepared in the best situation, for the use of the public authorities and persons of distinction.

Every preparation having been completed, the director or master of the ceremonies advanced in the open area to the front of the grandee's box; and after ample salutations and a short speech, solicited permission to proceed with the entertainment. Upon this, the assent was signified by the great man throwing to the said functionary the key of the gate opening from the bull's den into the arena, whence they are let out one at a time in succession, but never before the precursor has been killed or removed from the arena; nor until the animal about to be bated has been well goaded and rendered quite furious by every sort of torment.

I shall not relate those details of the bullfight which have been so often and so perfectly described; I shall merely state that, thirteen bulls were tortured, one after the other, without killing any of them; the town, it was alleged, being too poor to pay for the bulls, and defray the expense of a *matador*. But as each bull in succession had been worried during a satisfactory length of time, he was turned out of the arena into the streets, through which he ran uncontrolled, with the utmost fury, until he reached the open country, every person not in the amphitheatre providing for his personal safety, by remaining a prisoner in a house.

As neither Williams nor myself had obtained leave to be absent during the night, we were obliged to retire before the conclusion of the fights; but we had remained so late, as to render it imperative on us to make good speed. We were, therefore, much disappointed, on applying for our horses, on being informed that the ostler was gone to the bull-fights, and had taken the key of the stables with him; he was sent for, and, although he came to us as quickly as could have been expected, yet this delay caused the loss of valuable time. Moreover, on entering the street leading towards Gibraltar, we found it to be so steep, and the pavement so much broken up, that we considered it would save time to lead our horses down; but this also increased our difficulty in regard of time, and for which we had made no provision.

Accordingly, we dismounted, but had not proceeded far down the hill, when some persons called to us from the windows, in a slang sort of language, to hurry on for fear of the bulls: thinking this was said in a joke or through a disposition in these people to amuse themselves at the alarm they expected to create in us, we advanced with unaltered pace ; at the next moment, however, we heard loud and reiterated shouts behind us, from all the upper windows of the street, and on looking around we observed a furious bull bounding from side to side of the narrow street, and tossing his head in every direction, whilst his tail was lashing violently in trying to tear out twenty to thirty barbed darts sticking around his neck and shoulders: his movements were so wild, and his rush so determined, that we forgot the steepness of the hill, the bad state of the pavement and the narrowness of the street; and having mounted, we were off at a gallop in the twinkling of an eye.

My expectation was, that I should thus merely change the manner of being killed,— break my neck instead of being ripped up and tossed a half-dozen of times in the air, by this tremendous bull; my surprise was therefore particularly agreeable on finding myself in a few minutes safe and sound on my horse's back, at a full gallop, and a mile a-head, at least, of the charging enemy. I know nothing of Williams's feelings on this occasion, for we exchanged not a single word; yet I should think they must have borne a strong resemblance to my own, since I found him close up with me, and we did not relax our pace until we had safely entered on and passed the draw-bridge at Land-Port.

We learnt afterwards that the bull, from whose horns we had so fortunately escaped, had been considered to be the finest of the lot; for, prior to being turned out of the arena, he had ripped open a horse in the most splendid style, and had very nearly killed the rider, by tossing him into the air to the height of fifteen to twenty feet; upon which the whole of the audience bestowed on him the loudest *vivas*, and most thundering applause, clapping of hands, waving of handkerchiefs, &c., all of which must have been highly satisfactory and particularly grateful to the wounded man, whilst he was carried off streaming with blood, writhing with agony, and groaning to the entire satisfaction of the ladies and gentlemen of every class.

CHAPTER VIII.

The Orion returns from Messina—The Author consents to dine on board with Ellers—The torture he endured—Danger of being carried off to Sea—The difficulty of escaping from the Orion—Landing from a launch—Rozia Bay—Rather queer sort of work, but ultimate escape.

ABOUT this time, the Orion returned from Messina and Malta, having left General Fox and family at the former place, and now Ellers passed almost every day with me on shore, as he had entirely recovered his former good health. After a short delay, the Orion was appointed to sail Westward, with the first favourable wind; and, as her destination was reported to be the West Indies, Ellers begged of me as a particular favour that I would dine with him on the following day, " since," added he, " it may be a long long time before we meet again, God knows; perhaps never in this world."

I consented, although very reluctantly, on condition that I should on no account be detained on board during the night, having, as he well knew, a great objection to sleeping on board, and more especially on this occasion, when the Orion was under orders to proceed to sea, with the first change of wind.

Accordingly, on the following day (1st of September, 1806), at about two o'clock, I went to Ragged-Staff, intending to hire a boat to carry me off to the Orion; but I there found Captain Joyce, of the navy, commanding the Camel store-ship, with whom I was well acquainted. Joyce very obligingly offered me a seat in his boat, and to put me on board. On our way I asked Joyce his opinion as to the stability of the wind, then blowing a stiffish breeze from the Westward, and I was relieved from some anxiety by his assurance, that he thought there were no indications of a change.

On reaching the ship, I met with the

heartiest welcome, and nothing was wanting to make the time pass most agreeably. Ellers was seated at the head of the table, and did the honours in such good style, that the hours were short and sweet. I, nevertheless, observed with some uneasiness the declining daylight; and I reminded Ellers of his promise to have me put on shore before it should be too late; to which most of the officers replied, " Plenty of time yet;" but soon afterwards, as we were drinking a sort of farewell toast—" Pleasant passage, and plenty of prize-money to the Orion; and may we all meet again soon, and pass another happy day together, no matter in what quarter of the globe," which was echoed by several, I heard the evening-gun fired on the top of the rock.

Ellers suddenly became very serious and uneasy, the others winked at each other, the officer of marines looked wise and said nothing, whilst the First Lieutenant seemed to take no interest in the event, but seized his hat and went upon deck. The boatswain's whistle piped away repeatedly, and from the noise and general bustle, I became alarmed;

and in reply to my inquiry, I was very coolly informed that every boat belonging to the ship was at that moment hoisting in.

"And how am I to get on shore?" was my first and most anxious question. To which I was answered, it would now be impossible for me to leave the ship before morning gun-fire.

"But," said I, "suppose the wind should change in the night?"

"Oh, never mind about that, there is not the slightest chance of it; you shall have my cot," said Ellers.

"We shall make you as comfortable as we can," all exclaimed; "and in the morning there will be no lack of boats to put you on shore, as early as you like *after gun-fire*."

"I'll not risk it for any thing upon earth," cried I, somewhat warmly. "I'll go to the Captain, and state my case; and surely he will not refuse to allow me to be put on shore."

Upon this I was told that the Captain had gone to dine on shore, and the hour of his return was quite uncertain; and, for the first time, I now learnt that the Captain and his officers were on bad terms, and that there was not an officer in the ship would dare to ask him for any kind of favour. The hoisting in of the boats at evening gun-fire, they said, was observed with the most rigid punctuality, and no shore-boat was allowed to communicate with the ship after that moment.

Whether this severity was practised because the ship was about to sail, or not, I cannot tell, but such was the case on this occasion. I was greatly vexed at being thus caught in a trap; I felt that I was taken in, which always produces an unpleasant feeling. I gently reproved Ellers, and he readily admitted that I had great cause of complaint, which he deeply regretted; but he assured me that it was without design I was detained, for the gun had been fired much before he had expected it.

We now adjourned to the deck; the wind was still fresh from the West, but as the last gleam of light faded away, the wind also, as is usual in this climate, greatly diminished. Ellers and myself walked up and down, conversing on the chances of our meeting soon again, and on the numerous changes to which we might be subjected during that time. In speaking of his intended marriage with a very amiable girl (now Lady Napier), the sister of Captain Younghusband, of the Royal Artillery, he dwelt with delight on his anticipated happiness.—" My dear little Eliza and darling children dancing about me, when shall we next meet ?" were ever uppermost in his mind.

With these and similar pleasing dreams of the future, the evening glided away until past nine o'clock, when a man-of-war's gig pulled up swiftly to our larboard side. The boatswain's mate was instantly at his post, sounding his pipe, two men over the side holding out the man-ropes, and the officer and midshipman of the watch at the gangway ; all the other officers on deck stood back. In an instant the Captain stepped on the deck, the sentinel presented arms, the officers saluted with their hats, whilst the Captain, with proper dignity, raising his hat, passed on quickly to his cabin, without addressing a single word to any body.

On discovering that it was the Captain who was coming up the side, I expressed a determination to lay my case before him, and request that a boat might be ordered to put me on shore. But Ellers and all the other officers declared that it would not forward my wishes, and would have no other effect than to augment that want of harmony betwixt them and the Captain, which already existed to a very inconvenient extent.

I, therefore, abandoned that intention, and immediately ran to the gangway to beg a passage of Captain Stewart, then commanding the Sea-Horse, who had just put the Captain on board, and with whom I was acquainted; but here I was again foiled, for the gig had pushed off at the instant when the Captain of the Orion had quitted her, so that he was now half-way to the Sea-Horse, lying two or three cables' length to the Southward.

The arrival alongside of the gig had raised in me most sanguine expectations; the severity of my disappointment was, therefore, greatly increased by the failures I had just experienced; no hope of getting away from the ship before morning could be cherished, and my fate must now depend entirely on the stability of the wind during seven or eight hours longer.

"Seven or eight hours," partly addressing Ellers, and partly communing with myself; " seven or eight hours is a long time to depend on the continuance of the fickle wind from the same point of the compass, particularly when a person's future prospects may be totally destroyed by a change,—by a puff from the Eastward all my expectations in life may be blasted, and I may be ruined for ever."

I had pronounced the last words in a tone manifesting so much despair, that my inward agony had become visible; upon which Ellers, grasping me by the hand, and in a half-soothing, half-jocular manner, said:

"Come, come, my dear fellow, cheer up your spirits, you might just as well jump overboard at once as to go on conjuring up all the possibilities without regard to the probabilities! Hang it, man! if we sailors were to rack our brains in search of all the possibilities, you would never get another ship to go to sea."

Several of the officers standing round joined Ellers in his efforts to dispel the gloomy state into which I had fallen, when one of them exclaimed:

"You are right, my boy," slapping Ellers on the shoulder. Then, turning to me, "*Nil desperandum* is my motto, pray what is yours?"

"*Siempre pronto*," replied I.

"Indeed, always ready," giving the English translation, which, as my motto was Spanish, I did not expect. "Then we'll try your practice against your preaching, supper has been waiting this hour or more, come, let's go to work."

"You're a cup too low," said Popham.

"Half-a-dozen, I think," cried Julien; so down to the ward-room we dropped like a deep sea-lead.

Although but ill disposed to sup, I took a little cold meat in compliance with the pressing instances of my friends; after which, it was proposed, and unanimously hailed with satisfaction, and, no doubt, with much sincerity, that we should drink to my safe deliverance from on board of the Orion on the following morning.

Having received a hearty shake of the hand from all around, I retired to Ellers' cabin, and in a few minutes had jumped into his cot.

Again left to myself, my mind relapsed into its previous state of anxiety; I had been in hopes of taking some rest, yet my sleep was like that of the grenadier, who sleeps with one eye whilst he watches with the other. In this way I heard the ship's-bell striking every half-hour; but by degrees, as the hours passed on, although each appeared as long as a whole night, I went on plucking up a little. Four bells, or two o'clock, were now struck, which greatly revived my spirits; I began to view my past alarm with some ridicule, and I fairly began to slumber. At this moment I was startled by the shrill sound of the boatswain's whistle, followed by three heavy stamps with his foot. Then, oh! I shall never forget it, with the loudest, hoarsest, and most sepulchral voice I have ever heard, he thundered out, "All hands to get under-way!" and to prevent any chance of being misunderstood, this he thrice repeated. I was absolutely petrified, and for some seconds believed that I must have been dreaming.

All the inconveniences, mischiefs and horrors I had painted to myself, on contemplating the risk of being thus unexpectedly carried off, perhaps, to the West-Indies, and which I had but a few minutes before discarded as mere possibilities, now rushed back upon me with double force, almost depriving me of the powers of reason. I hurried on my clothes, and was dressed before I was aware of what I was doing. Then rushing out for the deck, I met my good friend at the cabin-door, who came, he said, to save me the unnecessary trouble of getting out of bed.

He treated my alarm as quite uncalled for, and although he freely admitted that the wind was fair and strong from the Eastward; "Yet," said he, "the cables are twisted, and it will require at least four hours to clear them and get under-way; by that time the morning gun will have been fired, and plenty of shore-boats will then ply about the ship; so compose yourself, my dear fellow!—turn in again and finish your dream, whilst I keep a sharp look-out on deck."

To this advice I could not yield, so went on deck with Ellers.

The people were all up, and many of them on deck engaged in making the various arrangements necessary on going to sea; whilst a large number below had manned the capstan, and were stepping round, marking the time with their feet to a merry tune played on the fife. Every man seemed to be actively employed, yet but very few words were heard; even the orders of the officers were not delivered in a louder voice than was indispensably requisite to secure their being clearly understood.

The silence and steadiness of these movements were better calculated to irritate and heighten my distress than to induce a more composed state of mind.

Every officer on deck had a duty to perform, which fully occupied his attention; they had, therefore, no leisure to sympathise with me, nor even to offer me a word of consolation. Ellers, it is true, did his best; and although he continued to assure me that no doubt existed in his mind that the morning gun would be fired long before the Orion could start, yet his manner was so agitated, and his answers, at times, so confused, that I clearly perceived he was not, himself, perfectly convinced of the accuracy of those assertions.

A whole volume might be filled in attempting to detail the mental agitation I suffered during the operation of getting the ship under way.

"I have not mentioned to any one living creature," thought I, "my intention to dine on board of this ship; what confusion, therefore, the discovery of my absence will create! Messengers sent in every direction all over the Rock and into Spain, will return without procuring the slightest tidings of me; the various precipices at the back of the Rock will be searched in the expectation of finding my mangled carcase." I then just recollected that I was in orders as President of a regimental court-martial to be assembled at nine o'clock that morning. "I may, perhaps, be suspected of having deserted to the enemy!" This thought absolutely made my blood boil. "I shall be advertised in the 'Gibraltar Chronicle,' and a reward offered to any one who shall give such information as may lead to the discovery of my body, dead or alive! This will reach England—my family will be plunged into the deepest affliction,—all my effects at Gibraltar will be sold,—my pay will be stopped,—my name struck off of the list of the corps of Royal Engineers,—my vacancy be filled up; and, in short, for the next four months at least, I shall be regarded and treated as one no longer belonging to this world."

During this highly excited, and I may say, frenzied state of mind, I stuck close to the officer of the watch, that I might obtain the earliest information of the progress making in clearing the cables, which every now and then was reported to him. These reports were more and more unfavourable to my interests, since they represented the work as proceeding much quicker than Ellers had thought possible, and that the ship would very soon be ready to make sail. Every report of this nature pierced me like a dagger through and through. I looked at my watch, then to the Eastward, still no symptoms were visible of the first dawn of day; by my watch another half-hour must pass before the gun would be fired. I now began to count the minutes, when the anchor was reported to be atrip, that is, only waiting for the last heave to separate it from the ground. I turned in breathless agony to the officer of the watch, entreating he would delay for half an hour, nay, one quarter of an hour, the final order.

"It is more than I dare comply with; I have, believe me, every disposition to oblige you, but it is more than my commission is worth."

"So long as there is life there is hope," thought I, as I cast another anxious look towards the East, where I saw, or fancied I saw, the first peep of day.

> "There's many a slip
> 'Twixt the cup and the lip,"

exclaimed Ellers, full of delight at a chance, however remote; and at which I caught as a drowning man would at a straw; for it was touch and go with me. Ellers now stepped up to the officer of the watch, and whispered in his ear; the officer turning round in haste, said, " You know as well as I do, that I dare not; I would do anything consistent with my personal safety to oblige you and your friend, but I cannot hazard my commission; you know, my dear fellow, that everything that passes is regularly reported by ———" I could not catch by whom, or to whom, these reports were made, for at that moment I felt a sharp tug at the skirt of my coat, and at the same time a fine little fellow, a midshipman, whom I had made to dine with me at the mess, on meeting him on shore some days before this, whispered in my ear that a man-of-war's-launch going on shore to water, was at that instant passing under the Orion's stern. I had not heard the conclusion of the officer's reply to Ellers, but I had caught enough to make sure that he had refused to delay the departure; and this supposition was immediately confirmed by his order to complete the heaving of the anchor, and set the fore-and-aft sails.

"By heavens! if I miss this chance, I am completely done for," I muttered to myself.

Not a creature had noticed the Middy's communication. I dogged the opportunity; and, in the twinkling of an eye, I was over the side and snug in the larboard main chains. There was by this time just enough light to enable me to discern the bows of the launch, peeping out from under the stern of the Orion, and a man standing up in her, fending-off from the ship with a boat-hook. Time was too precious to admit of hesitation, for the head of the Orion was swinging round, and in a minute or two more she would be running away in fine style before the wind. I, therefore, hailed the man with the boat-hook, and, in a tone of authority, ordered him to come alongside. "Ay-ay, sir!" was his reply; and, at the moment when she was nearly at the foot of the ladder, with her water casks piled up sky high, I heard the voice of the officer of the watch, in a hurried manner on deck, inquiring for the *soger-officer*, upon which the sentinel at the gang-way told him that I was in the larboard main chains. Ellers was immediately sent to see what I was about, and to bring me in. On reaching the gang-way, Ellers immediately twigged the launch, and, guessing my intent, entreated I would come in, adding, " Upon my soul! if you leave the ship before gun-fire, against the orders, the officer of the watch, the sentinel, and myself, may be severely punished for having connived, as it will be stated, at your departure; for God's sake! let me entreat you to come back on deck."

" And so commit an act next akin to suicide," replied I. " By the Lord Harry! I'm in no such humour—the swiftest and nimblest must have it," was my reply, as I ran down the side of the ship, with the speed of a squirrel; but as the launch was by this time a couple of yards, at least, from the side, pushing off in obedience to the sentinel's orders, I turned my back to the ship; and, gathering all the elasticity in my power, I took a desperate leap into the boat, not caring much on what or on whom I might fall. "The risk of breaking a leg is nothing to getting away from the Orion," thought I, as I sprang from her side.

A voice, as loud as thunder, ordered the launch to put back—upon which I ordered the contrary. "A gallon of rum to you, my lads, and plenty of backy; pull away; pull like devils, I say; pull your arms off. Never mind what they say, don't you see they are off to sea;—they are bound to the West Indies—they will never trouble any of you— they don't know to what ship you belong— pull, I say; pull like———" and pull they did, with all their strength.

The Midshipman was a nice boy, only, as he afterwards told me, about twelve years of age, and he made no resistance to my desire, for he had been affronted, he said, by some of the Orion's people, and was not anxious to oblige them, so he made no effort to return, seeing that the ship was actually making way. At this moment the officer of the watch, I suppose, hailed, and declared he would fire into the launch, if we did not immediately put about; upon which I could not refrain from replying by such a gesture as should prevent the possibility of any one mistaking my contempt of the threat; and, as I was perched up on the top of the highest cask, the advancing daylight rendered it, no doubt, very visible on board of the ship. In an instant, to my surprise, a musket was fired, but without effect, and almost at the same moment the gun on the top of the rock announced the return of day.

I now repeated my exhortations to the *Jolly Tars*, reminding them of the promised rum and backy, which produced such pulling, that our speed almost equalled that of a gig; and, at the same time, the sails of the Orion having caught the stiff breeze, we were out of reach of hailing and of shot in less than two minutes. I never met with Ellers after this; he went to England, married, and died, leaving, I believe, two children.

Although I have never had an opportunity of hearing the result, if any, of my departure from the ship, so contrary to the efforts of my friends, nothing serious, I should think, can have happened to any of them; and, as to the shot that was fired, I have no doubt that it was carefully directed to pass at a respectable distance over our heads.

I was soon landed in a small bay South of the New Mole; to this place the water from the great Navy tank is conveyed in pipes, and thence into the casks, without removing them out of the boat.

On looking about, I found myself hemmed in betwixt the sea on one side, and a semicircle of inaccessible rocks on the other, projecting into deep water at each extremity of the bay, and, at least, thirty to forty feet high. "How am I to get into the garrison?" I inquired of the sailors who had brought me on shore. They looked at the cliffs, then at each other, for they at once reflected that to get the rum and backy, I must be got up and within the walls. One of them pointed to a small wooden building, only a few feet square, which I had not before observed, and which stood perched up, like a sentry box, on four posts, which rested on the beach, and exactly as high as the rocks, and from which a narrow bridge extended, to a small opening in the thin parapet wall, bordering the edge of the cliffs.

The man said, that he himself would not be much troubled at how to get in, for he should climb up by one of those posts, in which spikes at regular spaces up to the top had been driven by the sailors, so that they might go in and out of the garrison, whenever they were sent for water; "but," scratching the back of his head with his right hand, as he lifted up his hat with the other, " I don't know how it would agree with your clothes and hands, for that place, as you may suppose, is none of the cleanest in the world, I can assure you."

Making a virtue of necessity, and still almost jumping out of my skin on thinking of my lucky escape from a forced and most disagreeable trip to the West Indies in the Orion of seventy-four guns, I carelessly observed that, to avoid any dispute, I must insist on having every man belonging to the launch, present on the top, at the time when I should deliver to them the promised reward for their services. The sailors readily agreed to my views, and by this ruse I conceive the way had been cleared of the reputed annoyances, as I reached the top, although last, by no means the least satisfied; for the circular dimensions of several of these jolly fellows greatly exceeded mine.

Having thus fulfilled my engagements by providing the stipulated articles within a few doors of the house occupied by Mrs. Cox, I hastened to my quarters, and found no difficulty in attending the court-martial most punctually.

CHAPTER IX.

The 13th of September—Floating Batteries—Rejoicings on this Anniversary—St. Michael's Cave—Loss of the Athenian, a very authentic account—Lieutenant-General Sir Hew Dalrymple arrived—The Marquis and Marchioness of Santa Cruz, Colonel Stirling, and Bagpipes—Mr. Wilson, a Jeweller from Lisbon—A Topaz Suite for an English Countess—The Countess de Noaïlles—Major Bryce.

THE 13th of September was a day much celebrated at this period, being the anniversary of the destruction of the floating batteries, which had been constructed by Monsieur D'Arson, the French engineer, during the memorable siege, expressly to form a breach in the sea-wall of Gibraltar; and they were purposely built to resist red-hot shot, and the bombarding with heavy shells, the former, it was said, by water circulating through the timber-framing, which, it was confidently asserted, would effectually protect those vessels against being fired by hot shot; and the upper decks being covered with a steep roof, made of strong timber, would secure them, it was expected, against danger from heavy shells. And as these batteries were furnished with cannon on one side only, a good deal of internal contrivance in the ballast was required to provide a satisfactory counterpoise.

Notwithstanding such an ingenious arrangement, these floating batteries, placed opposite to the King's Bastion, at the distance of eight hundred to nine hundred yards, were very soon set on fire by red-hot shot; and after burning for some time, six of them blew up.

By this result, so contrary to the expectations of the allied armies of Spain and France, a great number of lives were lost, notwithstanding the gallant and very intrepid exertions of the garrison, who fortunately succeeded in rescuing a great number of the

Spanish Artillery-men on board those vessels from a watery grave.

Such was the result of this great event, which is said to have saved the fortress of Gibraltar from returning under the Spanish dominion; it is not, therefore, very extraordinary that the anniversary of that day should be celebrated and regarded as one of general rejoicing there.

Amongst the various amusements was that of visiting St. Michael's Cave, which, on this occasion, was lighted up with a great quantity of torches; whilst ropes and rope-ladders were fixed throughout its intricate labyrinths, and attended by soldiers of the corps of Royal Military Artificers (now the Sappers and Miners), well acquainted with the necessary precautions to be observed in descending.

These preparations invariably attracted a vast concourse of persons of all ranks and of all nations, and commonly were productive of much amusement.

It was generally supposed that the cave descended to the level of the sea, or about a thousand feet, at least; but no one had ever been certain of having reached the bottom.

Accordingly, on the morning of that memorable anniversary (in 1806), I went up to St. Michael's Cave, which is situated at no great distance from the Southern pinnacle of the Rock, on which is a tower, partly destroyed by lightning, called O'Hara's Folly; and I had formed a determination to descend to the lowest and farthest extremity practicable. On my reaching the entrance, I heard loud bursts of laughter and shouts of merriment, which I soon ascertained proceeded from a crowd of people assembled around two officers, who had just returned from a voyage of discovery down the cave, and who were now perfectly covered from head to foot with black and very offensive mud.

I must admit, that the besmeared appearance of those officers was by no means calculated to strengthen my determination; 'and after a short conversation with one of them, I perceived that my desire to fathom Saint Michael's Cave had entirely left me; and, I think, it would have been somewhat difficult to have revived that ambition.

Several dinner-parties at the Governor's, and at the military messes, at the principal inn overlooking the Alameda, and balls were patronized, in order to keep alive the happy recollections of the memorable 13th of September, 1782.

The Athenian of sixty-four guns, Captain Rainsford, with whom I was on terms of friendship, being on the point of sailing for Sicily, Lieutenant Mulcaster, of the Royal Engineers, who was under orders to proceed to that island, requested me to endeavour to procure for him a passage in the Athenian; he cared not, said he, in what part of the ship, were it even in the main-top, so anxious he was not to delay his departure. I immediately saw my friend Rainsford, and pressed a compliance with Mulcaster's wishes; but Rainsford's promises were so numerous, that he assured me "he had not a spare plank of his cabin floor to offer him."

With grief at heart, and sorrowful eye, poor Mulcaster saw the white sails of the Athenian spread to the breeze, and shape her course round Europa Point; and was reduced to the misery of embarking on board the first transport ship that sailed up the Mediterranean, some ten or twenty days after the Athenian's departure. Here he felt the loss of all those conveniences and comforts of a ship of war, in lieu of which he was allowed the run of the cabin exclusively to himself, and which provided him with a substantial oak table and benches, and nothing more; since every officer was obliged to supply whatever else he might please to have in addition. Not one cup, plate, dish, knife, fork, glass, nor earthenware, stone ware, nor iron ware of any description, table cloth, or cooking utensils, were provided for him; if sufficiently fastidious to think that any of those luxurious articles were necessities, he must put them on board, or economise their cost and do without, and live upon the uncooked ship's ration.

The Athenian had a prosperous run, until on the 20th of October (1806), being then on the North side of the island of Sicily, when, at half-an-hour past ten o'clock P.M., Rainsford having spread his chart on the table, and with an opening in his compasses, representing forty miles, he placed one point on the Squirks, (rocks, the existence of which had been up to that time very much doubted,) and extending the other point either to the North or South, I do not know which, he said to those around the table, "There, gentlemen, is the exact position of the Athenian;" and at the same instant the ship, with a terrific shock, struck and stuck on the very Squirks he had calculated to be at the distance of forty miles off, and very soon afterwards foundered. The launch, which is the largest boat in every ship, was thrown into the sea with the least possible delay, and therein one hundred and fifty-five persons were saved, out of about five hundred, the number on board at the time of striking on the Squirks. Captain Rainsford did not leave the ship; the launch rowed round to the stern, and he was thence hailed, and desired to jump overboard, in order that he might be picked up and saved; and it remained uncertain if he heard the summons, but he did not jump overboard as entreated by his friends in the launch; and it was believed that, having frequently expressed much doubt, and even a disbelief that there were such rocks, more particularly on the morning of the fatal day, he did not wish to survive the loss of his ship. Doctor Pymm, now Sir William Pymm, was, with General Campbell, and others, passengers in the Captain's cabin, and were saved in the launch. Pymm suffered a severe loss, in all of about one thousand two hundred pounds, of which eight hundred pounds' worth was in Spanish dollars. Rainsford had been occupied in drawing up his instructions for the ceremonies to be observed in the celebration of the first anniversary of the victory of Trafalgar, which was on the following day.

So far as I have above narrated of this melancholy and disastrous event, I have every reason to believe it to be a faithful record of the particulars, since they were communicated to me by one of the highly respectable individuals who had been on board at the time of the wreck. I have not, however, the same guarantee for the accuracy of the sequel, for which I am indebted to general rumour, as follows:—

It was asserted, that one of the Lieutenants of the Athenian observing a boat pushing off from the ship, after she had sunk with the deck nearly level with the sea, attempted to leap on board, but treading on a rope as he made his spring, the rope slipped from under his feet, and he fell violently on his chest upon the gunwale of the ship, and before he could recover his footing, the boat had gone too far for him to repeat the attempt, but in a few seconds she sank with every one on board, and they all perished; the officer, it is presumed, escaped to the launch, and was thus most providentially saved. And I hope Lieutenant Mulcaster, who had grieved so much at being disappointed of a passage on board the Athenian, felt the powerful interposition of his Creator in his behalf.

In the November following, Lieutenant-General Sir Hew Dalrymple arrived, having been appointed Lieutenant-Governor, and superseded the universally respected Major-General James Drummond, who, on the departure of General Fox, had assumed the command.

The officers composing Sir Hew Dalrymple's staff were his son, Captain Dalrymple, of the 15th Light Dragoons, Military Secretary, and Captains Blair and Gubbins, Aides-de-camp. Although no very great alterations were made in consequence of this change in the person of the Commander-in-Chief; yet, a more rigid observance of the King's regulations in regard of dress was enforced than had been required by Generals Fox and Drummond. These trifles are, however, of little moment at this distance of time.

In the early part of the following month (December), the Spanish Marquis and Marchioness of Santa Cruz, both young, and the lady exceedingly handsome, paid us a visit; and I was appointed by Sir Hew to escort them, show them the lions, and, in short, to be with them constantly in order to secure their meeting with no interruption nor want of proper respect; for they were grandees of the highest class and immensely rich.

The retinue consisted of three Spanish

officers, serving as Aides-de-camp or Equerries, and two ladies' companions or of honour, all young and good looking.

The first day was devoted to an inspection of the lines and galleries along the Northern face of the Rock, leading to St. George's Hall, and thence South by the roads passing Bruce's and Ince's farms to St. Michael's Cave, and from that place down to Windmill Hill by the Mediterranean Stairs; and so on to the New Mole, home by the Saluting Battery. The ladies had been provided with donkeys part of the way, yet they were exceedingly fatigued, and, although they now and then expressed some approbation, none of the party appeared to me to be more than commonly pleased.

We all dined with a Mr. Vialé (afterwards Sir Emanuel Vialé), an opulent Genoese merchant; and on separating for the night it was agreed that the following day, instead of being employed in continuing the inspection of fortifications, of which they seemed to have had enough, should be devoted to the far more interesting occupation of shopping; for the Spaniards are not unlike the people of other countries, they are fond of every thing which is dear or scarce in their own country; and gladly eatch at an opportunity, such as the one now possessed by this party, of purchasing English articles of dress, stationery, hardware, &c., at about half, or even, perhaps, one-third of the prices demanded for the same in Spain.

These grandees and their friends made very large purchases; and passed but few shops unnoticed, commencing with Waring's, linen-draper, hosier, mercer, &c., and Holmes' pickles, sauces, and Hambro'-beef shop, both in South Port Street; then Gordon's tin and copper goods warehouse, and Breceano's Italian warehouse, both near the Spanish church; Wilson, silver-smith, jeweller and trinket cutlery, in the Alameda; Miss Graham's, millinery and dress, opposite to Bedlam; and although last, by far the most important, the very celebrated Toledano, they afterwards took ices at Madame Passano's.

The quantity of goods purchased were all sent to Vialé's, and would have been enough wherewith to open business in Spain; and the excellent bargains which, in their opinions, they had secured, put them in the best possible humour. The party now retired to smarten up a little in order to partake of a *dejeuner-à-la-fourchette*, to which they had been invited by his Excellency, Sir Hew Dalrymple; who had also engaged the whole of the aristocracy of the place to meet these noble visitors.

On approaching the gates of the convent, the guard on the opposite side, facing the entrance, mounted on that day by the 42nd Regiment, turned out and paid the grandees the same honours as are due to our Field-Marshals, that is, presenting arms, officer-saluting, regimental colours dropped, and music playing a march.

The music on this occasion was performed on the Highland bag-pipes, which sounded away gaily to the ears of a Highlander, but to the Spanish Marchioness appeared to be so defective, that as I held her arm in mine, she whispered to me, "*Ave-Maria purissima, que maldito instrumento!*" then adding, "I should like to hear one of those things played upon when in proper tune;" whence it was evident that she considered the discordant sound proceeded from the instrument being a bad one of the kind, and much out of tune.

Colonel Stirling, who then commanded the 42nd, a thorough Highlander, was close to me at the time when the Marchioness spoke so disrespectfully of the Highlander's favourite, and which, at his request, I related to him. Stirling, greatly incensed at this, quickly exclaimed, with considerable energy, and which he expressed in his usual broad Scotch accent, " Hang her bad taste for music ! tell her that if she canna admire the bag-pipes she's no worthy of the honour done her this day by the 42nd pipes, nor of any further nautis ;" upon which Stirling walked away, and took no further *nautis* of her during the rest of the day.

The breakfast was very splendid, and the grandees departed for Spain, highly pleased with the reception they had met, and assured me of their desire that I should, by paying them a visit in Spain, give them an opportunity of manifesting how greatly they felt obliged to me, personally, for my unceasing attentions to their wishes during their stay at

Gibraltar. Some years after this period, the Marquis having died, and the Marchioness being then the Governess of the present Queen of Spain, I addressed her a letter, requesting a favour of her, reminding her of our acquaintance in Gibraltar, &c.; but she very coldly, and very briefly, replied that she never interfered in matters of that nature, without any recognition of our having met at Gibraltar, or of her pressing assurance of services. Lieutenant-Colonel Ramsay, of the Artillery, having returned from a trip to Lisbon, his account of the city, opera house, &c., together with the civilities he had experienced from some of the wealthy merchants to whom he had delivered letters, rendered us all exceedingly desirous to visit the capital of Portugal. He particularly mentioned a wine merchant, named Citaro, who had introduced him every where while at Lisbon. Ramsay had made many purchases of jewellery and trinkets, and among others, from a person named Wilson; and I believe it was through Ramsay's advice that this jeweller came to Gibraltar on a speculative tour. Wilson very soon displayed his valuable stock; every body hurried to make purchases of precious stones, "for," as a Yankee would have expressed himself, "half nothing." I was neither the last nor the first he contrived to plunder; for some articles which I purchased and paid five pounds, and even ten pounds for, on my arrival in London were calmly declared to be worth about as many shillings; the stones were, as frequently marked in London, "real stones," but the gold settings, an Irishman would have said, "were not gold at all;" a grain or two to an ounce, at most.

Whilst on this subject of Lisbon jewellery, I must be permitted to run a-head three or four years. On my leaving England in 1810, under a special commission from the King, and under the instructions of Lord Liverpool, I was entreated by a lady of high rank (a Countess) to purchase for her at Lisbon one of the handsomest suits of topazes, but very particularly that the whole must be set, for, added her ladyship, " they do those things so much better abroad." Her ladyship did not think of fixing the price. The final commission had not been given till I was handing her to her carriage, consequently, that most important part of the affair was left entirely to my own discretion. We thus arrived at the carriage, when her ladyship waved her hand, wishing me a pleasant passage and speedy return, and, " pray don't forget!" the carriage-door banged, and cut off all further conversation on the subject. Although I was under no anxiety about the financial part of the affair, yet I should have been better pleased to have had a price named as the highest.

When about to leave Lisbon, on return, I devoted an entire morning to the jeweller's shops along the Rua Aurea, and inspected all the topazes in Lisbon. I requested Colonel George Fisher, of the Artillery, a capital judge, to guide me in making a selection, but some duty prevented him. I was, therefore, reduced to the necessity of making a purchase on my own judgment. I finally bought a very handsome set, after examining every stone, separately holding it up in every position to detect defects, and paid down one hundred and sixty-five pounds. On my arrival in London, I was anxious to receive the opinion of Messrs. Rundel and Bridge as to the merits of my selection, and lost no time in finding my way to Ludgate Hill. I produced my red morocco case, and asked them if they could easily determine about the value of the topazes. After a few moments, without examining the stones as carefully as I had expected, one of them said, smiling at the same time,—" Yes; we can easily state the value of this set, for it is one we sent out to Lisbon a few months ago, to be sold to the English officers, whom we understand are good buyers of these articles at Lisbon. We could not sell them here, but there they do very well; our price was one hundred and twenty pounds." I shall keep to myself the mortification I experienced at having been so completely duped; and after turning the matter over in my mind a few minutes, I at length agreed to give my purchase, and fifty pounds more, for a very superior suite of topazes, with which the countess was exceedingly delighted, repeating twenty times over that she could not have procured one in this country, of equal merit for double the amount it had cost her.

Early in 1807 (about the end of the month of January or beginning of February), the French Countess de Noaïlles came to Gibraltar, attended by a man-servant only. She was direct from Madrid, and solicited permission to be allowed to enter the fortress, and view the fortifications, which Sir Hew Dalrymple very willingly granted; and I was again appointed to escort that lady. Before I commenced the excursion, I waited on his Excellency Sir Hew Dalrymple; and, in reply to my inquiry if he wished any part to be reserved, he said,—" Oh, no! show every thing; the more the enemy sees of this fortress, the less he will be inclined to meddle with it."

The Countess de Noaïlles was then about forty years of age, tall, and still a very fine woman; her manners indicated the refined education she had received, and dignity and nobility marked every one of her actions. Her man-servant, her only attendant, as I have just above stated, was in livery, and closely followed our steps; and with that familiarity not unusual in French servants, occasionally, but with the greatest respect, joined in putting several questions to me, regarding the fortifications, particularly as to their merits and peculiar objects; and the information he thus requested was so truly scientific, that I began to entertain suspicions as to his real capacity; and, instead of regarding him as a footman, I could not refrain from viewing him as an officer of Engineers. This caused me to watch him very closely, in order to detect if he made notes or sketches; and, although I could not perceive any thing of the kind, yet some small rolls of paper, which I observed in the succession of five or six little loops or folds in the silver lace round his hat, and which ascended from the centre of the front, tended to increase my suspicions, and I reported it to Sir Hew Dalrymple.

The first day was devoted to the works, extending from Land Port to the Rock-gun, including all the galleries. The second, from Land Port to the New Mole; and, on the third, we visited Bruce's farm, Ince's farm,

Pocoroko and St. Michael's caves, &c. At the latter, the Countess accepted some refreshments I had sent forward, and she appeared to be highly gratified with the inspection, and with the attention I had shown her.

On leaving Gibraltar in the afternoon of the next day, for Algeziras, she placed in my hands a letter for Lady Cahir, and requested I would forward it, which I failed not to fulfil; and she promised to write to me from Paris, and give me some information as to the fate of my mother's uncle, who commanded a regiment of Swiss guards at the commencement of the great revolution; and also respecting another relative then serving in the *gardes-du-corps* of Louis the Sixteenth, and belonging to the company of her father-in-law, the Prince de Pois; but I never heard from her, nor of her, after she left Gibraltar.

On the 10th of April, 1807, to my great surprise, as I was looking out of my window one morning, towards South Port, I observed an officer of Engineers enter the town, whom I immediately recognized to be Major Bryce. He had just arrived from England, and was on his way to Sicily, to relieve Captain Lefebre, the Commanding Engineer. I went out to meet him; and after the usual expressions of surprise and pleasure at meeting him so unexpectedly, I went with him to pay our respects to Colonel Fyers, where we both dined that day. Bryce dined with me at the mess on the following day, and proceeded on his way to Messina on the 12th, taking with him Lieutenant Harding of the Engineers, having brought with him an order to that effect from General Morse. I snapped at this opportunity to beg of him to request the Inspector-General of Fortifications to order me to proceed to Sicily, as it was then still understood that some expedition would shortly be dispatched from that place. Some time after this, I received a letter from Bryce, stating he had complied with my request and I received several letters from him, requesting me to render him some very interesting services at Gibraltar.

CHAPTER X.

Change quarters—Good garden—Colonel Fyers tries the change of air by going to sea with Sir George Cockburn, and finally goes to England—The Royal George, Sir I. T. Duckworth—Very polite reception of my visit—Stone shot and Maltese ass—The 6th Regiment arrived—Toss-up Toledano, a celebrated Jew.

ABOUT this time Captain and Mrs. Buchannan, of the Royal Engineers, sailed for England; and as the house occupied by them was very convenient, and I had a right to take possession of it if I pleased, I failed not to do so; particularly as there was an excellent garden, for Gibraltar, attached to it. These quarters were not, however, free from objection; for the Jews' Synagogue formed the boundary of the longest side of the garden which faced the house, and which contained most of its windows in the side next to the garden.

In the ordinary course of things, the removal of our furniture from one house to another is regarded as a sort of event, and generally produces an inconvenient derangement and confusion in all our little matters, during several days before and after. In addition to these annoyances, we, not unfrequently, have to deplore the destruction or mutilation of some valuable articles; but in military life we do those things very differently.

Having, *pro formá*, communicated my wishes to the officer commanding, with respect to my change of quarters, to which, of course, no objection was made; I sent my servant one morning, after breakfast, to the barracks, to order thirty or forty soldiers of my company, with three or four hand-barrows, and two or three carpenters, to come to my house immediately after dinner.

The party at the appointed hour marched up to my door, and six of them at a time entered the house; when each taking up a convenient load of carpets, chairs, or tables, &c., returned to the street, and there waited until the whole had in like manner received their portion to be carried, excepting the carpet bearers, who went on immediately; the carpenters taking down the curtains and bedsteads. In this way, every article in the house was distributed in light loads, and in a few minutes the house was perfectly empty. The serjeant having ordered each man to shoulder his share, he ordered the procession to march off by the right, and as the various articles which should be first put into the house had been made to move on at the head of the line, on their arrival at their destination they were all put into the best order at once. Thus, on the 20th of April, 1807, I completed the formidable operation of moving to a house, about a mile distant from the one I quitted, in the short space of less than two hours, by which time my bed was made, the washing apparatus ready for use, the pictures, about sixteen in number, and a looking-glass, all hung up in their places; my library, of upwards of one thousand volumes, had been carried in the same order, on the shelves, and all my linen had been left in my drawers, the whole without suffering the slightest injury.

I was now greatly delighted at having a real garden instead of an artificial one in boxes on the roof of a back kitchen; and, although it was of such dimensions as elsewhere would be viewed as being very small, yet at Gibraltar it was thought far from contemptible, being about seventy feet in length by about thirty in width.

My little orange trees which I had reared from seeds were now fit for transplanting, having grown up to the height of about two feet in little more than a year, and my lemon and citron plants were still more forward. I very soon received some important additions from Ceuta, and various parts of Africa, and my naval friends were very kind in bringing me valuable plants, seeds, and flowers-pots from Sicily and Malta; the pots from Malta are made of a very soft stone, and are beautiful, but in a short time after exposure to the atmosphere, they become very hard.

During many months prior to this period the health of our most excellent commanding Engineer, Colonel Fyers, had been suffering frequent attacks. He had already had the advantage of a trip to sea with his family on board of his friend's ship, Captain Cockburn (Sir George), which had been of essential service to him; he was, nevertheless, advised that his return to England would be highly conducive in restoring him to a more permanent improved state of health.

Accordingly, in the month of May, Colonel Fyers and his amiable family embarked for England, carrying with them the sincerest regards of every officer then at Gibraltar; and were followed to the place of embarcation by a vast concourse of the inhabitants, with sad faces and tearful eyes.

On his departure the Colonel made me a present of some splendidly sculptured vases, and many valuable flowers.

Captain Evatt now assumed the command of the Engineers until the arrival of Lieutenant-Colonel Sir Charles Holloway, who, it was understood, would not leave England before the arrival of Colonel Fyers.

About this time (10th of May, 1807), the Royal George, with Admiral Sir I. T. Duckworth on board, anchored in the Bay of Gibraltar on her way home, having been severely handled by the Turks in passing through the Dardanelles.

Lieutenant Mercer, of the Royal Engineers, having a brother on board, and who was well acquainted with the Admiral, invited me to accompany him in paying a visit to the Royal George, which I accepted.

We found the Admiral in full dress, ready to receive visitors; but he did not go on shore during his short stay. Sir I. Thomas Duckworth was a corpulent man, rather pompous, yet very courteous; and although rigged out as if he were going to attend a drawing-room, with silk stockings, shoes and buckles, and star and ribbon of the Bath, his hair dressed and well powdered, yet he offered and insisted on showing us round to every part of the ship; and with the utmost urbanity, explained the exact effect of each of the enormous stone shot that had struck the Royal George; marking out the extent of damage done by one in particular, which had entered the ship between the lower and main decks, nearly abreast of the mainmast.

Sir I. Thomas then showed us two shot, of coarse white marble, which had lodged in the Royal George; one of them measuring two feet eight inches in diameter, and of the weight, as he informed us, of eight hundred and twenty pounds, the other somewhat smaller. The Admiral also showed us a very fine Maltese ass, standing full sixteen hands high, the tallest I had ever seen.

The shot just above mentioned I have heard are placed on stone pillars, at the entrance to Sir Thomas's park, near Torbay, in Devonshire.

After partaking of refreshments, we took leave of the Admiral and of Captain Dunn, with whom I had been acquainted for several years. We returned to the shore much gratified at having seen the shot, and their effects; and also at the attention we had experienced. I believe the Royal George sailed for England on the 12th, and arrived after a very pleasant passage on the 26th of May.

Very soon after this, the 6th Regiment of Foot arrived at Gibraltar; and although many changes had taken place amongst the officers since I had left them in Canada in 1802, I had much pleasure in meeting my old friend, Captain W. McBean, now Lieutenant-General Sir William McBean. Colonel Foord Bowes still commanded the 6th, and arrived with them.

I had nearly omitted to mention one of the lions of Gibraltar, a Jew, whose celebrity for tossing up had spread far and wide, even to North America, where I had frequently heard his name mentioned on any one proposing to toss up.

Toledano was the man; and he kept a shop in the main street, on the right-hand-side in going towards Land-Port, and nearly opposite to a large house, late the European Hotel, but which, in 1807, and perhaps a long time before, had been hired by Government, and occupied as barracks for officers.

The goods kept for sale by our friend Toledano, were chiefly coarse Barbary shawls, belts, woollen and cotton cloths, silk kerchiefs, and night caps, of many colours, ornamented ivory fans, particularly pomatums, Cologne-water, attar of roses, combs, brushes, &c. &c. &c.

On entering the gloomy shop, the first distinct object that met my sight was a tall, skeleton-faced man, between forty and fifty years of age, with very small sparkling and sunken eyes, and a complexion somewhat darker than merely sallow. His dress consisted of a light brown or grey kind of dressing-gown, with loose dirty-white trowsers, and yellow morocco slippers down at heel, and cotton stockings, covering legs evidently too thin to dispense with the use of garters, an auxiliary, however, which he had never thought of much importance.

This was Toledano.

On perceiving us enter, he rose from his seat, in a dark corner behind the counter, covered with glass cases, and in three strides, passing round its extremity, almost met us at the door, with his never-failing smile on seeing a new-comer enter his shop.

My friend, Captain Skyring, of the Royal Artillery, introduced me with due pomp and ceremony, stating my ambition to have the supreme felicity of tossing up with him.

"Oh, sare, de honore vill be upon me; I shall enjoy very particular honore on dis occasion,—de signore Capitano dare," pointing to Skyring, " can say to you what great mans I have toss up. Now, signore, I toss for any ting you will speak, from one cob to one tousand cob, what much you say, eh?"

I was fully aware of the Jew's established practice on this subject, always to pay in goods, which he took care to value at double the real worth; but if he won, then he expected the amount in hard cash. This system upon the long run rendered his game perfectly safe, since it secured twenty-five per cent. in his favour.

Toledano repeated the challenge to name the amount for which we were to toss, when I proposed that it should be for a modest cob (the Gibraltar name of a Spanish dollar), and which I won. I was then desired to pick out any article I might fancy; upon which I selected a small bottle of attar of roses, and which he valued as the equivalent of a cob, although currently sold in the streets by the Moorish Jews for less than half that sum; but Toledano's attar was, no doubt, of a very superior quality.

It was part of this artful fellow's system to settle the account immediately after each toss; for had he acted otherwise, by allowing the debt to be settled after several tosses, he could not have secured the profit arising out of the difference in value of money and goods. Thus, for instance, when I had won a cob, he immediately paid me with goods not worth half a cob, and if I had tossed again and lost a cob, I should have paid a cob in cash, leaving him half a cob in pocket; but if the payment had been left unsettled until after I had lost the second toss, in that case my winning would have been cancelled by having lost the same amount.

Toledano now pressed me to toss again for

double the amount, but which, to his disappointment, I declined, postponing that honour to another day. Perceiving that I was immoveable in my determination, he presented me a large book, bearing the marks of age, and begged of me to sign it, an honour, he said, which had not been refused him, "as great deal of very great mans have sign de book as a toss-up vit de famos Toledano."

He now again begged very hard for "anoder litel toss-up, for no more dan two cobs;" and at this moment, the Civil Secretary, an officer of Artillery, holding a high and valuable civil appointment in the garrison, looked in, and gave us a nod, then passed on; upon which Skyring said, "That's the man, Toledano; he will toss-up with you for any amount you please, shall I call him in?"

"Oh, for my God, do not insult me by dat man!" replied the Jew; "dat man, Capten, sare," turning to me with eyes glittering with tears, and flashing angrily, "dat man rob me terribly! No, I beg his pardon, no, I do not mean rob, I want to say I was fool," evidently retracting the expression, lest he should have committed himself by an assertion too bold. "Pray, sare, never speak of dat man vit me. Oh, I shall not long forget how I lose my money! But, den, who was possible to suppose such a great gentleman as dat Captain?" half to himself.

In looking over the book, I observed the name of the individual above alluded to, and that of a great many persons of rank; some of them were merely passing a few days at Gibraltar, whilst on their way up the Mediterranean, or returning thence.

The extreme vexation manifested by Toledano at the mere mention of the individual above alluded to, excited in me some curiosity to be informed of the cause, which Skyring related as follows :

Soon after the arrival of His Royal Highness the Duke of Kent, at Gibraltar, as Governor, the gentleman in question visited Toledano, and was immediately invited to toss-up, which was accepted for the sum of a few cobs. "But," said the new-comer, "Mr. Toledano, I must teach you the fashionable manner of tossing-up now adopted, and which you will at once perceive is neater and very superior to the old clumsy way."

"What is dat way, Capten?" quickly inquired the unsuspecting Jew, anxious to be up to the newest and neatest mode of tossing-up. "You will do me de great honor if you teach me dat, Capitano,"—alternately using the Italian, Genoese, Spanish, and English pronunciation of Captain.

"Well, then," said the Captain, taking a piece of money from his pocket, and as it whirled away in the air, "Heads I win, Tails you lose, that's the way we do it; now, Mr. Toledano, how do you like it?"

"Oh, sare, dat is very pretty, I like dat very much," replied Toledano, quite delighted at the simplification.

"Then here goes; shall I toss, or will you, Mr. Toledano?"

"Oh, it is just de same, I tink."

Then up went the coin, whilst the Captain repeated, "Heads I win, Tails you lose," and up came Heads. The Captain having fairly won, the articles were immediately selected as payment, and were valued as fairly as usual;

and, as usual, Toledano, having lost, he pressed, with all his best rhetoric, to double the stake on another toss-up, but which was prudently and stoutly declined.

The book was presented and signed, and so it ended for that time. A few days afterwards the Captain called again, and another toss-up was offered and accepted, when " Heads I win, Tails you lose," was proclaimed to be the guide, as the very best, most convenient, and of all the ways the least open to trickery; but on this occasion up came Tails, when Toledano demurred; he was, however, at once convinced that he had fairly lost, on repeating in a half-whisper, " Heads I win, Tails you lose." A third toss was unluckily accepted by the Captain, and which began to open the eyes of the most celebrated tosser-up of his day, when he archly observed, " But when do I win, Captain?"—a difficult question to be answered without due reflection, thought the Captain; he, therefore, immediately recollected that he had a very pressing appointment with His Royal Highness just at that moment, which justified a very precipitate retreat; but as he hurried out, he promised to let him into that secret at his next visit.

After the Captain had departed, Toledano practised his hand at tossing-up in the best and most fashionable way, at every toss accurately calling out, "Heads I win, Tails you lose," when he very soon came to the conclusion that he had been *done brown*.

CHAPTER XI.

Bottles of Porter concealed—O'Hara in a difficulty—His various efforts to detect negligence in the military duty—Party to Algeziras hastily terminated—Spanish Marquis and the celebrated Marotti—A very unpleasant affair.

HAVING, on many occasions, when rambling over the upper parts of the mountain, experienced severe thirst, particularly during the Summer season—for there were no houses, or even a spring or fountain, where a drop of water could have been obtained in those parts—I resolved on forming little depôts of bottled porter, at such places and at such distances as should always put it in my power to procure the means of satisfying that distressing want. For this purpose, I rose before the sun, and, taking with me two or three bottles by degrees, in that manner I formed four depôts, leaving at each three to four bottles, and a tin tumbler.

One of these was in a very dark and cool situation, under the circular flight of wooden stairs, leading from St. George's Hall to the platform above; the second was behind a very remarkable mass of projecting rock about midway between the Rock Mortar and Middle Hill signal-tower; at this place was a recess, never heated by the sun, and which I kept blocked up with four or five large stones. The third was in St. Michael's cave, in a natural cavity, as well suited to my purpose as if it had been artificially formed. The fourth was in an exceedingly cool and well-concealed spot, within a few yards of the Mediterranean Stairs, and a little higher up than a Saint Patrick's cross, painted in red by General O'Hara, whilst he was Governor of Gibraltar.

The situation in which the General must have been when he painted that cross, is so frightfully dangerous, that it seems to be almost incredible how any person, but particularly a man advanced in age, could have had nerves strong enough to venture to descend to that spot, whence, however, he was unable to return without aid ; and as he had no one with him, it is related that he remained in that spot for several hours, when, fortunately, an Artillery drummer, who was passing up the Mediterranean Stairs, was hailed by the General, and ordered to procure him proper assistance, and not to fail sending a pot of red paint and brush, all of which was, of course, as quickly at the place as the distance could permit ; and it is asserted that, even with the use of ropes, some difficulty was experienced in rescuing the General.

Prior to my final departure from Gibraltar, the three first of my little hoards, as mentioned above, were exhausted, but two bottles of porter were left in the fourth, near the Mediterranean Stairs; and they were so well concealed, that I think it highly probable they have never yet been discovered.

These hidden treasures, for such they really were, afforded me on numerous occasions a vast source of amusement, in addition to substantial comfort; for it several times happened, that I escorted friends or others on their arrival from England, to show them the lions; and when suffering great thirst, I have sometimes asked them how they would like a glass of good English porter, and what they would give for it? This, no doubt, excited a still greater desire to moisten the parched state of their mouths, and would have been almost unpardonable, had I not been in a position to procure the liquid; I, therefore, waited, until near one of my cellars, and with due caution, to avoid disclosing the exact place, I gratified the desire I had so much increased. The surprise, delight, joy, and even raptures with which I have seen them gaze on a bumper of creaming porter, thus most unexpectedly held out, inviting them to appease the devouring thirst, beggars all description. I leave it to be imagined by those who have experienced a decided want of liquid to moisten a parched mouth, a suffering which few have escaped in a greater or less degree.

In mentioning the name of O'Hara, it brings to my recollection in the liveliest colours many anecdotes related of him, at the time to which I have just adverted, and which are strongly indicative of the eccentricity of his character and of his attachment to off-hand men and abrupt measures.

It was asserted that on a vacancy having occurred in his staff, an officer then serving with his regiment, stationed at Gibraltar, was anxious to be appointed the General's aide-de-camp; but having no introduction to the General, and no circumstance having brought him more under his Excellency's notice, than any other officer then in the garrison, he felt that none of the ordinary measures, such as memorials setting forth services, events, family connections, &c., could hold out to him any reasonable grounds for expecting to succeed.

This officer, however, appears to have caught at the true mode of proceeding with O'Hara; for, instead of puzzling his brains in drawing up a flowery and highly-wrought letter, he wrote to him nearly as follows :—

"Sir,

"I take the liberty of offering myself to fill the vacancy which has occurred in your Excellency's staff; but, as I am almost totally unknown to your Excellency, I shall, perhaps, be refused; yet, as I am determined ultimately to succeed, I shall prove myself to be deserving of it, when I am sure I shall be appointed accordingly.

"I have the honour to be ———."

O'Hara had frequently noticed the author of the above letter, as he marched past in mounting guard, and had formed a rather favourable opinion of him; and, on reading his letter, he immediately sent a message, desiring his attendance at the convent. On entering the room, his deportment was soldier-like, bold without being offensive, and blunt without rudeness; as he advanced, the General, in a loud and rough manner, said,—

"So, sir, are you the author of that letter?"

"Yes, sir," he replied, without shrinking from the responsibility, or noticing the offended air which the General had manifested.

"So, sir, it seems you are determined to be my aide-de-camp?"

"Yes, sir;" in a voice as firm as the General's, and in no degree daunted.

The General then, with affected submission, as one compelled to give way to a superior power, said,—

"Well, sir, if that is the case, I have no alternative; I may as well yield at once.— Certainly, sir;—to be sure, sir;—begin now, and send the town-major to me directly, that he may put you in orders;—bring in your baggage, and seize possession of your predecessor's room. I have no means of resisting it, so commence this day."

And so from that day he entered on the duties of aide-de-camp to his Excellency General O'Hara. O'Hara was a severe disciplinarian, particularly towards the officers, his favourite maxim being, "make the officers do their duty properly, and you may depend on it the soldiers will rarely fail to do theirs." On a special occasion, a great portion of the officers of the garrison attended a ball in the town, and kept it up to a very late hour, which occasioned many of them to be absent from morning parade, usually assembled at six or seven o'clock A.M., and, accordingly, reported themselves to be indisposed. Without much further inquiry, O'Hara gave out in the general orders of the day, that "His Excellency feels much regret at the indisposition of so many officers of the garrison; and being fully aware that their anxiety to return to their duty, might induce them to leave their rooms before they may be completely recovered, the General desires they will confine themselves to their respective quarters for the space of fourteen days." In plain words, they were placed under arrest during a fortnight.

It was said that O'Hara carried his military zeal so far, that he neither rested night nor day, his mind being so entirely bent on satisfying himself of the strictest performance and obedience to his orders; in short, I have heard it related at Gibraltar, by those who had served there under his command, that he had the shoes taken off one of his riding-mules, on purpose that he might go night rounds, and visit the guards in the most silent manner without being heard, until he was very near the sentinel of the guard.

I shall merely relate one more of the numerous stories told of O'Hara.

As had been the long-established practice, O'Hara always attended the guard-mounting parade on the sands, at six or seven o'clock in the morning; and he took so much notice of the officers of the several guards, as they marched past, that he could generally, during the remainder of the day, name the officer on each guard.

One day he was proceeding out of South-Port in his carriage, when he passed an officer going into the town, and whom at the instant he remembered as having passed in review before him that morning, as commanding the South guard. Upon this, the General immediately determined on satisfying himself as to the fact, and so convict him of the heinous military crime of quitting his guard, and ordered the coachman to drive with speed to the South guard. Away they went, at the rate of ten to eleven miles per hour, along the saluting battery; and, in a short time, the horses out of wind and covered with lather, reached the South guard, a mile or more from the place where the Governor had passed the suspected officer.

At the usual distance the running sentinel called the guard to "Turn-out," which was obeyed with all the alertness desirable; and the officer advancing, unobserved by the General, at a quick pace from near the carriage, drew his sword, then opening ranks, presented arms, and saluted in the very best manner.

At the sight of this officer, every doubt had been removed. "By Jove! it is he himself," thought the General, as he ordered him to turn in the guard, and beckoned him to come up to the carriage.

"Pray, sir," impatiently inquired O'Hara, "did I not see you but a few minutes ago walking very deliberately into town, near South-Port?"

"Me, sir?" with the greatest simplicity, and pretending great surprise at the question: "I am on guard here, sir."

"Well, well, I know that, sir; you need not have supplied me with that valuable piece of information. Did I not, sir, I ask you again, did I not see you going into town, as I came out by South-Port?" his Excellency raising his voice, and his face reddening with anger at the officer's attempt to conceal the fact by his evasive reply.

The officer after a moment, in no way disconcerted, nor showing any symptoms of timidity, looked the General full in the face, and then, with great politeness, said, "Will your Excellency have the goodness to state if that question is put to me by his Excellency General O'Hara, Governor of Gibraltar, or from yourself in the capacity of a private gentleman?"

The off-hand manner with which this question was put to O'Hara struck the right chord, when, after a few moments' hesitation, he replied, with a smile on his countenance, "Well, sir, as a private individual I wish to obtain the information."

"Then, sir, I freely confess that I did meet you at South-Port."

"Well, sir, that is honest. Now, sir, I want to know how the devil you could get here on foot as quickly as I did in my carriage, and that, too, without any discoverable fatigue?"

"Sir, I shall conceal nothing from you in the private capacity you have selected. On meeting you, I strongly suspected that you knew me; and when you stopped the carriage to speak to your coachman, I guessed your motive, so, feeling that if my conjecture were correct, I had no means of saving myself but by arriving at my guard at the same time as yourself, I got up behind your carriage, the only method left me of securing that object."

"By Jove! sir," exclaimed O'Hara, "I like your candour, and still more the dexterity and readiness you have displayed in extricating yourself from a position of the greatest danger, without which you would undoubtedly have lost your commission. I admire the man, who, when he gets into a scrape, can jump out of it at once. You must dine with me, sir, to-morrow," giving him a most hearty shake of the hand. "But take care, you must never leave your guard again; if you do, by Heavens! I'll break you."

It was about the commencement of the summer of 1807, that a party was arranged to take a trip to Algeziras, and that we should go thither by water, instead of the tedious land journey round the Bay. The names of the individuals who agreed to join on this occasion were, as nearly as I now can remember, as follows:

Captain and Mrs. Tonin, and Ensign and Mrs. Leraux of the 48th Regiment, two Miss Stanleys, Doctor and Mrs. O' Roarke of the Garrison Staff, Lieutenant Grantham of the Royal Artillery, Lieutenant Mercer of the Royal Engineers, Mr. Seager, a merchant, and, I believe, some four or five others and myself.

A handsome and capacious boat was engaged to carry us across the bay, and we all assembled at Water-Port by nine o'clock, fully provided in every respect for remaining at Algeziras during the night, in case of being unable to return in time to be admitted into the garrison. All had put on their merriest looks, and had resolved on rejecting anything that might lead to the slightest disagreeables, —the surest way of securing real enjoyment on such occasions. We thus pushed off, taking care to hoist a white flag, immediately on our advancing beyond the space usually occupied by neutral vessels, in order to protect ourselves from being fired upon from Port San Felipe, or from any of the other batteries along the coast, and on Pigeon Island, near Algeziras.

In this way we proceeded on a surface of an oily smoothness; and in the course of little more than an hour, we landed without any kind of obstruction from the authorities, excepting the showing of our special passport; but the shore is there so shallow, that a considerable degree of amusement was created by the various objections and alarms expressed by each of us on being carried to the shore.

A few of the officers of the party now separated from the others, to pay their respects to the Governor,—an indispensable formality on arriving in every garrison town; and during that time the ladies were most agreeably engaged in shopping. On rejoining them we lost no time in finding out our old friend Moretti, a first-rate composer and guitar-player, and a Captain in the Walloon-Guards: he was delighted at our arrival, and most gladly accepted our invitation to attach himself to our party.

We now commenced our rambles not only through the town, but extended our walks to the beautiful romantic scenery and gardens in the vicinity. I shall not attempt to describe the splendid prospects we enjoyed this day, from various spots overlooking the town and bay, with proud Gibraltar and its crowded shipping in the centre, and Ape's Hill and a long coast-line of Africa on the right, yet I well remember that we were all so much fascinated, and our thoughts were so completely absorbed in contemplation, that we forgot all else, till Moretti reminded us that the day was already so far gone, that unless we hastened away to the *posada* we should get no dinner. In Spain it is difficult to procure any cooking after the usual hour for dinner, until the time for supper approaches; the former was from one o'clock till three, or half-past, at latest, and during that time dinner may be obtained at a few minutes' notice; but after that, the servants, from the head waiter to the cook's mate, expect to be allowed the undisturbed enjoyment of the *siesta* until six o'clock.

On arriving at the *posada*, the tables in the coffee-room were all fully occupied, and it was not without much consultation and solicitations of some of the company, that we, at length, obtained the exclusive possession of an inner room, which was small, and just suited to accommodate us; and as there was no other communication with this room but by passing through the large saloon above-mentioned, our ladies, as English women, felt some hesitation on the subject, but soon perceived the necessity of yielding to circumstances; therefore, skipping across amongst the numerous company, chiefly Spanish officers, and, half-blushing, half-laughing, they, under our escort, obtained possession of the *cabinet de société*. In this apartment there were no openings but one window and the door by which we had entered, both of which, in consequence of the intense heat of the weather, were indispensably thrown wide open.

Amongst the Spanish officers seated at one of the tables nearly in front of our own room door, I quickly recognized a man whom Moretti had pointed out to me in the course of the morning, and had informed me that although he was a Spanish Marquis, he was only an ensign in the army. The age of the Marquis appeared to be about twenty-five years, and he was exceedingly corpulent for so young a man; his face in particular was large, with a full red beard and whiskers, which, together with a tendency to baldness, encouraged an idea that he might not be very unlike our King Henry the Eighth, when he had been of the same age. The costume of this creature was but ill calculated to remove the unfavourable impression which his personal appearance had at first sight produced, for his neck was bare, and the bottom of his shirt collar was tied with tape; his brown uniform coat being completely unbuttoned, exposed to view a shirt which some days before had been clean, and well plaited, and the total absence of a waistcoat revealed to our sight two braces of different coloured listing. On one side of him lay extended on the brick floor a cocked hat, so large in its dimensions that it created a fancy that he must have cried for one; and on the other side was carelessly deposited a cotton stocking, which evidently had been on bad terms with his washerwoman for some time past, but was now used as a fit substitute for a purse, and seemed to contain a very considerable sum of money, probably not less than two hundred to three hundred doubloons, or a thousand pounds. At the time when Moretti had pointed out this blade before dinner, he was carrying this dandy purse slung over his shoulder, instead of employing a porter, which its weight would have justified; and Moretti took that opportunity of informing me that this notorious Marquis passed his time exclusively in prowling about the town, frequenting the billiard tables and gambling houses, of which there were a great many; and he added, " Dat rascal is de tereur of de plas; he has fight a hundred time, and his arm is like de bar of steel, for no body can drag de sword from his hand, nor turn it side ways, while to kill him." So much for Moretti's talent in the English language, which was tolerably fair for a man who had never been in England, but had picked it up in conversing with the officers stationed at Gibraltar.

On perceiving this eccentric animal, our ladies, in particular, eyed him with a sort of horror and disgust. Dinner was very quickly served, and all went on very pleasantly; Moretti's anecdotes, and the novelty to many of our circle was very interesting, since only a few of us had before this time visited Alzerias. The Spanish officers, professionally gallant, seemed to be exceedingly well pleased with the beauty of our women, which they most fully merited, and they employed many devices to attract their notice, which the open door facilitated. In the midst of all this satisfaction a piercing shriek was heard, so loud, that it produced a most perfect silence throughout the saloon and our smaller number, and Mrs. O'Roarke, pale as a corpse, was caught in the arms of the person sitting next to her, who thus saved her from falling on the brick floor. Mrs. O'Roarke had fainted, and, in all appearance, was lifeless. Moretti, who was seated facing our room door, which afforded him a full view of the movements in a large portion of the saloon, instantly slammed-to the door with some force, manifesting his irritated feelings; but at the next moment a violent blow was struck on the door, from the side towards the saloon, and which, it afterwards appeared, was caused by a tumbler, which some of the Spanish officers had thrown with great force against it. This unexpected event had well nigh caused a general fainting amongst the ladies; upon which, our friend Moretti sprang to the door, which he drew open to its fullest extent, and advancing fiercely a few steps, declared that whomsoever he should discover to have been guilty of so much impertinence as to throw the tumbler, and occasion such unmerited annoyance to the English ladies, should answer to him for such conduct. The words had scarcely quitted the mouth of the Captain of Walloon Guards when the Marquis instantly stood up, and with extreme *nonchalance* accepted the invitation, adding, " Our friends shall arrange the details."

Our first attention having been devoted to the ladies, and more particularly to Mrs. O'Rorke, we had the satisfaction to observe that she quickly recovered, and after some short time she was sufficiently restored to explain the mysterious cause of her alarm. In few words Mrs. O'Rorke stated that from the seat she had occupied at the table she had a full view into the saloon, and that immediately facing the door she had observed two officers sitting at a small table opposite to each other, whom she had noticed to be fencing with their forks across the table; but that, although it had afterwards become evident they were merely in play, probably with an expectation of thus attracting the attention of our ladies, yet she had at the time believed they were fighting in good earnest.

It is almost unnecessary to add, that all our anticipated pleasures and amusements had fled. The prospect before us was gloomy in the extreme; the death of our good friend Moretti seemed to be inevitable, and our sole occupation was to consider and devise the best course we could adopt for preventing the intended meeting. It was well known that Moretti was a good swordsman—at least so we were informed by some of the Spanish officers with whom we had a slight acquaintance; but another observed, "It is equally well known he is no match for the Marquis, who has never failed to kill his man."

After giving the subject the benefit of our best and united consideration, and keeping in view we had been the innocent cause of the pending duel, and reflecting what endless mischief and inconvenience might emanate from such an affair, we formed the determination of stopping any further proceedings, by at once communicating the whole to the commanding officer. The result was, that both the Marquis and Moretti were ordered under arrest; and, after much parleying and frequent consultations, it was finally settled that the Marquis, attended by an officer on the staff of the garrison should wait upon us, and apologise to the ladies for having caused them so much alarm; and that Moretti should pledge his word of honour that he would never again renew the quarrel.

These negociations had occupied our whole evening and much of the following morning; and, immediately after the above apology had been made, and the affair thus terminated, we hastened away to Gibraltar, which the General had pressed, having, as he said, reason to apprehend that a certain number of malcontents would challenge every one of the gentlemen of our party, if we remained during the evening.

CHAPTER XII.

The night-blowing cereus rather expensive property, and very shameful behaviour of the company—The ghost of Lieutenant Hunter of the 42nd Regiment—Attacked with cholera.

I OFTEN eyed a deserted plant in a flower-pot left to shift for itself in a corner of the little triangular terrace in front of the Royal-Engineers' mess-room, and where, also, some officers were quartered, which I had often eyed wistfully. This plant somewhat resembled a cucumber, with one end stuck into the ground, and appeared as if it had never been watered or attended to in any way. Upon inquiry, no one owned it; so, on leaving the mess that evening after dark, I carried off this poor plant under my arm. The kind treatment it now experienced produced a very rapid alteration in its appearance, and I soon ascertained that I had very unexpectedly obtained possession of a great treasure, for it turned out to be the night-blowing cereus. The growth of this plant was truly surprising, for in a very short time it extended over a large space of the Southern wall of my house.

At this time it had become fashionable, with many officers and their ladies, to take great interest in the rearing of flowers, and very particularly in the blowing of this rarity; I was, therefore, solicited from all quarters to send due notice of blowing, or of the prospect of blowing, of the little wonder of the day.

One morning, the first bud, which had been forming during many days, began to enlarge so much, and to open a little at the point, that I felt it my duty, in compliance with my promises, to send out the circular.

As dusk began, the company dropped in, each bringing one, two, or three very particular friends, with many apologies for taking such a liberty, and to each of them in return I expressed my obligation for procuring me the opportunity of making such an interesting acquaintance. Thus, instead of twelve or fourteen, I had more than double that number of visitors. They amused themselves as well as they could, and some of them took it by turns to watch the opening of the bud. By nine o'clock some further appearance of expansion was eagerly reported; but at ten and half-past the bud remained perfectly still; wine, fruit, and cakes, with some sandwiches, were handed round, and by eleven all expectation of the expansion of the bud on that night was abandoned; when my company dispersed, greatly obliged to me for my kindness, and with many and repeated assurances of being with me punctually at sunset on the following evening.

At an early hour next morning, before I had completed my toilet, I ran into the garden to look at the bud, half desirous of finding that it had blown and withered during the night. I was not so fortunate, but it had assumed a decided appearance of opening forthwith. "Well," thought I, as I went on finishing the operation of dressing, "the valuable flower which I have regarded as a great bargain, having obtained it for the mere trouble of carrying it home, is likely to cost me five pounds;" but I was doomed to pay for it handsomely.

In the evening, the whole of the party again made their appearance, and, to my dismay, with a great many additions; and again expressing a hope that I would forgive such a liberty, in consideration of "the great interest the individual takes in all botanical curiosities, and this is so rare a treat." Others, on introducing their friends, said they felt a great pleasure in bringing together two persons so devoted to scientific researches; and in a whisper, "My friend is a very learned man, and has often expressed a strong desire to form your acquaintance; he is dreadfully modest, but improves very much upon acquaintance; I am sure you will like him, and thank me for the introduction."

I was necessarily quite seduced by such flattering compliments, and it was impossible for me to omit immediately expressing my grateful acknowledgments for so distinguished a favour; and that I thought myself highly favoured by fortune, in being the possessor of a magnet so powerful as my night-blowing cereus had already proved itself.

Notwithstanding appearance, my flower played me the same trick as I had suffered the preceding day, and by about twelve o'clock, after refreshments, the whole of the amateurs, and those who merely came out of pure compliment to me, had retired, giving me the strongest assurances that they would be punctual on the following evening; for, although many of them had accepted of invitations to dinner and to evening parties, yet there was no sacrifice they would not make to gratify their desire of being present at the blowing of this very splendid flower.

I shall merely add on this subject, that on the third evening a still greater concourse of scientific and unscientific amateurs had been introduced, actually filling my little garden to a crowded state; when, to the excessive joy of all present, the blossom expanded very rapidly at about eight o'clock, and displayed all the beauties so justly attributed to this flower.

Although I had spared neither trouble nor expense to entertain the parties during three succeeding evenings; yet, on the morning following the last, I discovered that all my ceuta pinks and rarest flowers, some of which I had procured with labour and at a high price, and which I had watched with great care and anxiety, to see them bloom in the first style of perfection,—the greater part of these, but particularly all the best of them, had been most unmercifully gathered, perhaps by some of my scientific, but certainly by some of my very John-Bull-like visitors.

In order to publish and mark my indignation at such conduct, I caused a hand-bill to be put up at all the usual places, offering a reward to any one who should enable me to detect the offender or offenders. As I had expected, no informer claimed the reward; but I gained my principal object, which was to prevent a repetition; and the flowers were no doubt immediately destroyed; for, although I paid my respects on the following day to almost every individual who had been at my house, in the expectation of seeing my property ornamenting the table, not one did I any where discover.

A few days after this, the weather being exceedingly hot, I set out to take an early walk before breakfast. With this intent, I went out at Landport, and then by Forbes' Barrier and the Devil's Tower, and very soon found myself in Catland Bay, beyond which I was in hopes of picking up some mineral or vegetable curiosities.

The morning was, like all summer mornings at Gibraltar, during the absence of an Easterly wind, delightfully agreeable, though hot; the sky cloudless, and not a breath of air stirring. I sauntered onwards, my eyes cast on the ground, examining every pebble as I passed them, and with my small basket in one hand, and a hammer in the other, having a broad fan-like claw, resembling the ace of spades, to rake up plants with, or to break stones with the opposite side. My hat was pulled down as much over my eyes as possible, to screen them from the almost horizontal rays of the morning sun; my view was thus eclipsed of distant objects, excepting when I raised my head. In this way, my thoughts quite abstracted from the rest of the world, I proceeded, having seen nothing living on the wide, extensive, and smooth sandy beach of Catland Bay.

It was under all these circumstances, whilst a most profound silence prevailed, that I was roused, and, I will add, startled, by a loud voice, hailing me by my name in a broad Scotch accent, followed by a heavy groan. I jumped round at this, thinking the sound had proceeded from some one overtaking me; but my readers may judge of my amazement, when I could not discover a living being in any direction. During this surprise, the voice again addressed me in the same manner, and again appeared to come from behind me. I was now more perplexed than before, and looked in every direction, thinking it might be an echo, and that the person calling to me might be concealed at the foot of the cliffs, a thousand feet above the beach; for to that extent, in every direction, there was not any object of sufficient magnitude to conceal half the bulk of a man.

My anxiety was now excited to the highest degree, for the voice had sounded as from a person within ten to twenty yards of me; yet

I was about the middle of Catland Bay, close to the margin of the sea, and could discover nothing on the sands excepting the waved line of sea-weeds, chips, corks, and such other matters as are generally found on every sea beach, marking the extent to which the last high tide had reached.

Whilst staring about me, without omitting to look on the surface of the sea, the oily smoothness of which could not have concealed a chestnut, I was again addressed by the mysterious voice, which commenced by a deep hollow groan, and then said, " My dear fellow, it is the spirit of your late friend Hunter, of the 42nd Regiment, who was last night murdered on these sands, and whose body lies buried within a few yards of the spot on which you stand, that now addresses you. I want you to return without loss of time into the garrison, and acquaint Colonel Stirling, my late worthy Commanding officer, with my fate, in order that my corpse may be removed and interred with military honours. During my whole life I have always regarded that last ceremony with pride in my heart; and now my spirit hankers and craves after it more than you can believe; and it can never rest until that mark of respect shall have been manifested towards my remains."

This address, it will be readily credited, raised in me such sensations as I had never before experienced. The voice was familiar, and, undoubtedly, that of Hunter, then the Adjutant of the 42nd. I remained incapable of action, my mind strangely bewildered; and I believe that I had just made up my mind to ask some question of the invisible spirit, when I again heard the voice say in a plaintive tone, and evidently issuing from the ground near me, "If you have any doubt of the fact, go on thirty yards further to the South, where you see that biggish stone; behind it you will find my clothes, and the spade that was used by the assassin to dig my grave!"

I there, as directed, instantly found the articles named, which I most freely admit alarmed me exceedingly; and I really began to waver in my disbelief of the spirits of the departed revisiting the world. Just at this moment I observed an officer's servant advancing from the rocks at the Southern extremity of the bay, a hundred and fifty yards distant or more, and I hastened to meet him with all convenient dispatch. The man seeing me running towards him, hurried forward, and in a couple of minutes we met, upon which the servant hastily begged to be informed if his master required his assistance. Again I stared at the man, and asked him, whom I knew to be Hunter's servant, "Where the devil is your master?" at which the man laughed, and replied, "Why, there, Sir," pointing to the sands near the marks left by my feet, and just at the spot where I had heard the voice;

"What can all this be about?" replied I. "I cannot see your master, he is perfectly invisible to me; can you see him?" I quickly observed.

"Why, yes, Sir, *I can*, he is just under that bunch of sea-weed you may see yonder," replied Sandy; so leading the way, he took me to the very spot where I had been so unexpectedly hailed by Hunter's ghost, and on lifting up a handful of sea-weed he uncovered his master's face, who, as may be expected, burst out laughing, as he desired his man, Sandy, to dig him out.

I must now explain that Hunter was a Lieutenant in the 42nd Regiment, and during a long time had been a martyr to a general rheumatic attack. Hunter had been advised to try the effect of sand baths, which was the cause of my finding him on his back buried up to his ears; and in order to defend his face and eyes from the burning rays of the sun, he had directed his man to cover his face over with a light sprinkling of sea-weed, which did not prevent him from being able to peep through the weeds. Before this, Hunter was unable to stand upright, and his walk resembled that of a man one hundred years of age; but having persevered in the sand bath system, he ultimately was completely re-established in health.

During the latter part of the month of July (1807), I was invited to pass the evening at the South-guard, with Captain Blosset, of the 10th Regiment of Foot, where I met several officers and their ladies, with whom I was acquainted; and after playing at whist and round games, we had some cold meat and fruits, after which I took a glass of port wine negus. Having passed a very agreeable evening, at near twelve o'clock, when the grand-rounds were expected, we all departed.

We were a large party, most of us proceeding into town; and as Doctor and Mrs. O'Roarke, and Lieutenant Ferguson, of the 42nd Regiment, were quartered in a large building, lately the European Hotel, at the Northern extremity of the town, and my house was not far distant from thence, by the time we had reached our residences the company had gradually dropped off, and the individuals above-named and myself were the last left together; we now wished each other a good night, and separated in perfect health and spirits. I retired to bed, according to my constant custom, without the attendance of my servant; for the doors at Gibraltar were usually left unfastened during the night, burglaries being quite unheard of; and by burning a lamp in the hall I spared my servant the necessity of sitting up to let me in and furnish me with a light.

I quickly got into bed, and was off to sleep in a few minutes; but before two o'clock I was awoke by the most violent pain, just on the margin of the ribs, and a little below the pit of the stomach; which, however, occasionally for a moment or two left me. Thinking that I must have eaten something which had disagreed with me, although I had scarcely tasted any supper, I groped about in the dark, somewhat assisted by the light of the moon, and after some time I found a bottle of brandy, of which I drank a glass or two quite pure. The vomiting and pain continued unabated, and I drank another glass of my first-rate French white brandy, all of which produced no salutary effect; but the pain was evidently augmenting. I had laudanum and opium, and having lighted my candle, I went on taking fifty drops of the one, and then a pill of the other; and this I repeated several times. During the whole of that time I continued ringing my bell, at short intervals, in the hope of rousing my servant, but without success.

In less than half an hour I felt so alarmingly ill, that I went to my servant's room, in an out-building, and discovered that he was not in the house. I had now full need of summoning all my courage and remaining strength, for I was rapidly sinking, and in that condition started to procure medical aid. To friend O'Roarke I went off, and although his quarters were distant not more than two hundred yards, I twice sank with pain to the ground, or rather on the pavement. O'Roarke was up in a moment, and assisted me to return to my house, which, I am sure, would have been more than I could have accomplished alone; and his servant followed close on our heels.

More opium and a strong dose of calomel, then castor-oil and coffee, were all administered without any discoverable result. The agony I suffered went on increasing. Thus, in the short space of two hours I was reduced to so low a condition, that I could not rise in bed without aid. Severe spasms now attacked me, with cramp in my legs, soles of the feet, and palms of the hands, and a blue tint surrounded my mouth and eyes, and my pulse had almost totally ceased to beat. O'Roarke, at these symptoms, entertained but a very faint hope of saving my life; but determined to leave nothing untried which could hold out the slightest chance. He ordered a large kettle of boiling water, and dipping some flannel waistcoats therein, which he ordered to be applied, dripping with boiling water, to the pit of my stomach and parts adjacent, a considerable blister was very speedily raised.

Even to this day I well remember, that although the pain of scalding, as may be easily imagined, was severe, yet its effect was so soothing to the interior, that I rejoiced at the occasional removal of the cooling flannel, and the application of the one in its place boiling hot, so distinctly did it relieve the torture I suffered.

By degrees the pain and other symptoms abated, so that by nine o'clock I was totally free from suffering; but I was reduced to a state of prostration so complete, I could not speak without great difficulty, and was perfectly helpless; but in the short space of four days I was again on my legs, and at the end of a week or ten days more, was perfectly recovered. O'Roarke was, most deservedly, much praised for having saved my life, contrary to the usual result under all the circumstances of the case.

CHAPTER XIII.

The Garden Fête, good, but bad—The Prospects of a Siege—His Excellency Mr. Elliot—The Garrison is blockaded—Sir Charles Holloway arrives—Increased Forces arrive—Silver Spoons—Prices greatly augmented—Sir John Moore—General Beresford occupied Madeira—Speculations on the intended operations—Occupation of the Island of Perexil and its advantages—Major Burk—Ceuta is supposed to be the object of attack—The Author volunteers his services to Sir Charles Holloway to serve in any Expedition, and so does Mercer.

I RECOVERED from this severe attack of cholera in good time to lend my feeble aid in making some considerable preparations for a *fête champêtre*, meditated by Mrs. Evatt, and for which the garden attached to the residence of the Commanding Royal Engineer was well calculated. Captain Evatt's occupation of this house was temporary, being merely for the purpose of repairing his own proper quarters near South-Port, and until the arrival of Lieutenant-Colonel Sir Charles Holloway, the newly-appointed Commanding Engineer.

Accordingly, I now attended daily to various very ingenious devices which Mrs. Evatt had designed for providing little apartments, and alcoves for the refreshments, and to form concealed recesses for the bands of music; also to the preparations of the illuminations, and of triumphal arches, covered with variegated lamps, &c.

At length the much-desired day arrived, and all Gibraltar was there; even some of the merchants were invited, particularly the amiable, truly excellent, and most worthy Cardozo, generally denominated the King of the Jews, and who at that time was in the zenith of his glory, rich, highly-esteemed, and respected by all classes, and, of course, much courted; but many years afterwards, he died *poor* and *deserted*.

Every arrangement for the entertainment of the company was as perfect as circumstances could permit. The music could not fail to be very good, as it consisted of two military bands; the refreshments were provided without regard to expense, and well selected; the ices and cool drinks by Madame Passano, and the pastry by Celestine.

The dancing was kept up with great spirit until lamps and lanthorns were no longer required to illuminate the garden, or for the company to find their way home.

Nothing had been wanting on the part of the hostess that could contribute to the comfort, pleasure, and amusement of the company.

On retiring, I congratulated Mrs. Evatt on the perfect success with which, in my opinion, all had gone off. Yet the world at Gibraltar was exactly like the world everywhere else; no one felt grateful, no one praised anything, nothing was good, agreeable, well-managed, or as it ought to have been; in short, some said Mrs. Evatt had failed in everything but in gratifying her own vanity.

On the 27th of August, General Fox and

family arrived in the bay from Sicily, on their way to England; but as I was then confined to my house in consequence of a swelled face, they sailed before I could do myself the honour of paying my *devoirs* to that truly amiable family.

For some time before this, the French invasion of Spain had commenced, and rapidly spread its *anti-anglican* effects throughout the Peninsula: such, indeed, was the overwhelming influence, or, rather, the thundering will of Napoleon at this time, that our friendly intercourse with Spain by land was daily suffering additional restrictions.

We now began to regard a siege of this great fortress as by no means improbable; and many individuals made various private arrangements to meet such a contingency.

Some time before this, I had purchased several very splendid models, made of cork, representing some of the famed temples at Rome, by the celebrated Chichi, and which had been captured from the French by our cruizers, and sent into Gibraltar to be sold. These, I learnt, formed part of a present destined by Napoleon for the King of Saxony. In June, 1807, Mr. Elliot, our Ambassador at the Court of Naples, remained at Gibraltar for a few days on his return to England; and his Excellency obligingly took these valuable articles under his charge, and delivered them in perfect order to their address in England.

In August following, the rumours of a siege were greatly increased, nay, I should have said, almost confirmed, by our observing the Spaniards actually engaged in disembarking one hundred and sixteen twenty-six pounders on the beach, in the direction of Algeziras, not more than three miles from Gibraltar, and which had been brought in small craft along shore from Cadiz.

Many other movements were noticed from the elevated parts of the rock; and numerous reports, many of them, no doubt, greatly exaggerated, daily augmented the alarm; so that, in a short time after this, several families began to think seriously of preparing their departure, and a few ladies actually did take themselves off to England and Malta.

By the 15th of October, 1807, the most

vigorous land blockade was established; not a letter or even a newspaper was allowed to pass from one side to the other; and the advanced sentinels on the Neutral Ground were pushed much nearer to the fortress than had been hitherto practised.

It was in the midst of this new state of things, that Lieutenant-Colonel Sir Charles Holloway arrived with his family, to replace Colonel Fyers; and in the latter part of November, or commencement of December following, Sir John Moore, with about seven thousand men from Sicily, anchored in the bay. With this small army there came Captain Burgoyne, and Lieutenants Harding, Boothley, and Mulcaster of the Royal-Engineers.

The arrival and stopping here of such a force, the destination of which was not publicly known, gave rise to very numerous speculations as to the intention of government.

The addition of so large a number of officers, rendered the garrison exceedingly gay; many entertainments were given, parties and balls in rapid succession; but this enormous increase of visitors to our scantily supplied market, an evil greatly augmented since the communication with Spain had been closed, raised the price of every article required for the table, to more than double its already extravagant scale; thus, meat was not to be had under two to three shillings per pound; fowls ten to fifteen shillings each, and ducks the same; turkeys two to four pounds each; and eggs and cabbages one shilling each; and, in short, all other articles in the same proportion.

At one of the public balls above-named, and given by Sir Hew Dalrymple, I had been dancing during the greater part of the evening; and at near midnight, I was thinking of retiring, when I put my hand into my skirt pocket, to draw out my handkerchief, upon which, to my unspeakable surprise and horror, I found two silver tea-spoons, which I immediately produced to several persons with whom I happened to be in conversation. It will be readily imagined that I felt highly indignant at that event, for I have not the least doubt of its having been done by some villain, with an intention to ruin my character. Every one around me declared, in the most solemn manner, their entire innocence of having, in the remotest way, participated in this diabolical act, or of having any knowledge of the culprit. Unable to trace the author, I was compelled to remain satisfied, with giving the utmost publicity to this event before I left the ball-room. The spoons were small and old-fashioned, and on the handle of each was an embossed head or face very much raised.

At length, in the course of December, Sir John Moore sailed; and, as it was known that the French had seized on Portugal, this force was reported to be intended to take possession of Madeira. I believe this was really the intention of Sir John Moore, but he was relieved from the carrying this service into effect, by Major-General Beresford's expedition from England for that purpose, and which he accomplished amicably on the 24th of December, 1807.

During the winter and spring of 1808, troops continued to arrive from England, and were as quickly hurried off to Sicily; these were a part only of a much larger force which had sailed from England, but which shortly afterwards had been dispersed by a succession of severe gales; upon this occasion many of the transports foundered, and all on board perished; a large number had put back into Portsmouth, Plymouth, Falmouth, and Cork; whilst a few had managed to complete their voyage to Gibraltar, and, as above stated, had gone on to Sicily.

In one of these ships my friend Captain G. Harding, of the Royal Engineers, had arrived; and as he did not proceed to Sicily, I gladly gave him a share of my house.

These movements established a very strong, and I may add, a well-founded belief that there was something in the wind, as it is vulgarly expressed.

Many highly ridiculous and very far-fetched schemes were asserted to be the secret intentions of government, for assembling a larger force than usual at Gibraltar on this occasion; and which, with the utmost gravity, were repeated from mouth to mouth, as having been obtained from the fountain head.

The troops that had sailed up the Mediterranean, were now hourly expected to return into the bay; and their having been sent off, was treated as a mere blind to cover their ultimate destination.

Another expedition to Egypt was freely talked of by the knowing ones, but those who were supposed necessarily to know all about it, and yet who really knew no more than the rest, put on a very reserved air, answered no questions; but whenever any one broadly asserted that Ceuta was to be attempted by a *coup-de-main*, they smiled on one side, half winked on the other, and hastily walked away, nodding a "good morning to you," as if fearful of being unable any longer to preserve the secret which they did not possess.

The prevailing idea certainly was in favour of the attempt on Ceuta; and I am still of opinion that the attack on that fortress was, during some portion of the period in question, very seriously considered.

A small uninhabited island called Perexil, was taken possession of about the month of

February or March, and this greatly tended to strengthen that conjecture.

This little island is situated on the coast of Africa, at some distance West of Ceuta, and within less than half a mile from the foot of Ape's Hill. A small garrison, with Captain Fanshaw, of the Royal Engineers, took possession, and immediately fortified it, which was quickly accomplished, the coast being naturally very difficult of access.

The occupation of the island of Perexil, independently of any views upon Ceuta, was, however, of much value in affording greatly increased facilities for protecting our mercantile shipping, and it was, therefore, I believe, retained in our hands until the termination of the war with Spain in the month of June, 1808, following.

At length, about the end of the month of April, or commencement of May, Major-General Brent Spencer arrived at Gibraltar with a small portion of the original force that had sailed from England, under his command in the first instance, and which now amounted to no more than about four thousand men.

These troops were not hurried off to Sicily, as had been those which had arrived before them; but they remained at anchor in the bay; and this immediately revived the most active speculations, as to the ultimate object of the expedition; and such was the general fermentation excited on this occasion, that immediately after the breakfast hour was over, until dinner-time, every officer was busily engaged in news-hunting, first at the reading-room in the garrison library, then along the main street, the Alameda, the New Mole, Ragged-Staff, &c., and every one inquiring of the first he met, "Well, what news? has anything fresh transpired?" From this, none were exempted.

It was in the midst of this period of anxiety, either at the end of April or commencement of May, that one morning after breakfast, it was whispered about the town that during the preceding night a Major Burk, an English officer, had been admitted at Land-Port, not, of course, without previously reporting his request, and obtaining the sanction of the Commander-in-Chief, who ordered the Town Major to let down the draw-bridge for that purpose; and that after a short conference with his Excellency, the said mysterious individual had been put on board one of His Majesty's ships of war in the Bay, and had, without the delay of a moment, sailed, it was conjectured, to England; but nothing certain about this transpired.

This affair, as may be reasonably expected, excited the keenest desire to learn more on the subject; no other topic was talked of during the day; the mouths of those about head-quarters were double-bolted; and as nothing was declared from the Convent which could furnish grounds for founding any satisfactory calculations on this affair, invention stepped in, unopposed, and flourished in the wildest schemes.

The Captain of the Land-Port guard, who had received this Major, was hunted and tormented to tell all he knew about the matter; and any one who really had had direct communication with him, and therefore had obtained the best information out of head-quarters, was regarded as peculiarly fortunate;

and was listened to with nearly as much interest as the trumpeter's wife in Laurence Sterne's tale of Slawkenbergius, when she related all the particulars she knew in regard of the stranger's nose as he entered the gates of Strasburg.

Several years after this, when in conversation with Lieutenant-Colonel De Bourg, late of the 2nd or Queen's Regiment of Foot, I happened to inquire of him if he had ever seen the fortress of Gibraltar; upon which he observed that he had passed through that place during the night, on one occasion, in the year 1808. After some explanation, I observed that the only person I had heard of as having passed through Gibraltar at night in that year, was a Major Bourk, or Burk, but that I had never heard of him since.

"Why," said De Bourg, "I am that man. Bourke was then my name, but on becoming the elder member of the Clanricard family, I was permitted to take the name of De Bourg in lieu of Bourk; and which my brother, General Count Bourk, in the French service, still retains."

He then mentioned that on the occasion in question, he had just arrived from Madrid, where he had been secretly employed, and was then hastening off to England, in order to communicate matters of the highest political importance.

The assault on Ceuta was now more confidently asserted than before; and I was again determined on making another effort to be employed against the enemy. In this state of mind, one day, as Lieutenant Mercer of the Engineers and myself, were walking together near the garrison library, we met Sir Charles Holloway. After exchanging some unimportant observations, the military movements were next mentioned, upon which, Sir Charles, looking very wise, asked us what we thought was intended to be done; upon which we both declared our total inability to decide that all-engrossing subject; and we added, that every one believed it was intended to make an attack upon Ceuta; and I immediately seized this opportunity for soliciting, that should any officer of Engineers then at Gibraltar be appointed to proceed with the expedition, I might be considered as a volunteer to be so employed; and that I should be ready to start at a moment's notice; that my offer was not confined exclusively to an attack on Ceuta, but without reserve, on any service that might be contemplated; upon this, Lieutenant Mercer made the same offer of service, when Sir Charles said, smiling, " Well, gentlemen, I shall keep your requests in mind;" and so we very shortly afterwards parted.

Having already before this occasion volunteered three times my services on any expedition that might be in contemplation, without in any case having been successful; I now entertained but little expectation of being employed on the expedition then preparing to sail; and thus in a few days I had almost totally forgotten my offer of services.

CHAPTER XIV.

Very suddenly ordered to embark—Attend to the shipping of the stores—Captain Morrison appointed to embark to command the Artillery — Lieutenant Mercer and myself embark—Departure from Gibraltar with an East wind sometimes more difficult than might be expected—The guitar.

ALTHOUGH I devoted a good deal of time to pleasure, I nevertheless almost constantly employed a professor for my improvement, or to enlarge my acquirements.

To this end, during the first portion of the time whilst at Gibraltar, I received instruction in the Italian language from a native of that country, named Morasca; afterwards, I endeavoured to acquire the talent of playing on the Spanish guitar, under the able tuition of Pagliare, an Italian; and on his departure for Cadiz I took lessons from Dominico, and then from Domingo, both of them Spaniards. I soon found out that I should never arrive at any degree of proficiency on that instrument, beyond the humblest mediocrity.

After this, I turned my attention to miniature painting, and in succession had the advantage of two instructors; one of them a first-rate artist, and who, in a short stay at Gibraltar, realized a considerable amount for portrait painting. This last occupation procured for me much pleasure, and I made some progress, both in copying some miniatures which had been lent to me for that purpose, and in drawing from nature; and at the time above mentioned, I had in hand four or five portraits, requiring but a few hours to finish them.

In consequence of this, on the 12th of May, 1808, immediately after an early breakfast, having no particular duty to attend, I went to work, fully determined that no circumstance of any description should divert me from my purpose; and, in order to secure the due performance of a determination so firm and so laudable, I gave my servant the most positive orders not to admit any visitors, or, indeed, any one.

I had not, however, been more than half an hour at work, when several applications were made for admittance; and I rejoiced at the precaution I had adopted, in being denied to all and every body. "These visitors," thought I, "are more numerous than I ever had on any former occasion." Towards a later hour the bell was in constant action, when, at about two o'clock, I heard the voice of Lieutenant Mercer, of the Royal Engineers, in the garden; and I heard him declare that he would come in and stop there until I could be found; adding, that messengers had been sent all over the Rock to find me, without any success.

Upon this, thinking that some extraordinary circumstance had occurred, I put my head out of the window, and called him to come up to me; when, with astonishment at discovering that I was not out, he exclaimed, "My God!

where have you been all this morning? every search has been making to find you. You and I are ordered to sail with Major-General Spencer this evening; and Sir Charles Holloway" (the Commanding Engineer) "must see you immediately, to communicate his orders to that effect."

It will be readily imagined, this very hasty departure was quite unlooked-for by me. I had a good house, much better furnished than many other officers possessed; and had invited a rather large party of officers and their ladies to pass the evening with me.

Captain Harding was staying with me, which I regarded as particularly fortunate, for I left him in charge of all, excepting a few articles of clothing.

On the receipt of the communication above stated, Mercer and I went to Sir Charles Holloway's house, and I immediately received his orders to place myself as Commanding Engineer under the command of Major-General Spencer; and Mercer was at the same time directed to proceed with me.

Having expressed my warmest gratitude to Sir Charles for this early attention to my request, I hastened back to my house. My first consideration was, to send for my linen at wash, and order that it might be brought home in any state, wet or dry. I then swept out of my drawers, by the lot, all kinds together, and forced them into three or four trunks; upon which, I jumped and stamped down the highest lumps, and so completed in half-an-hour as much packing-up as most people would think a good day's work.

Whilst this was going on, three dozen of port wine, and six dozen of bottled porter, were packed up, in conformity with my instructions to the mess-man. A corporal's party now came from the barracks, and carried off my baggage and sea-stock, the latter having been packed at the grocer's; as also six pigs, about three or four months old, which I fortunately had, all in good condition, were also sent off and shipped.

So little time had been lost, that by four o'clock I jumped into a boat at Ragged-Staff, and embarked; but as it was now ascertained that we should not proceed to sea that day, I returned to the shore, and sought out General Spencer, to whom I reported my appointment.

These hurried movements did not cause me to neglect the party I had invited; for I deputed one of the number, a Major White, of the 48th Regiment, whom I met in the street, to do me the favour of seeing the others, and acquainting them with my deep regret at being unable to receive them that evening.

The departure of the expedition being postponed until the following day, enabled me to purchase a mameluke saddle and handsome bridle, with holsters, pistols, &c. I also went to the Ordnance storekeeper, Mr. Pringle, and handed to him a list of such stores as I had ascertained were not shipped, but which I considered to be the *minimum* of what I should require. These Mr. Pringle promised should be ready for embarcation on the next morning, at six o'clock.

After settling these and many other matters, which occupied my time until a late hour in the evening, I went on board of the transport No. 287, and hastened to take some rest.

Before going to bed, I was informed that Captain Fauquier, commanding the Artillery, had been ordered to disembark, in consequence of having declared his inability to proceed with the expedition, and that Captain Hughes had succeeded him in the command, but was still on shore.

At five o'clock on the following morning, Lieutenant Mercer and myself went to the Ordnance Store House, near South-Port, and examined and sent off the whole of the stores, for which I gave the usual receipt, and ordered Mercer to attend personally to the embarcation and proper stowing away in the ship.

I now set out with a view of taking my breakfast with my friend Harding, whom I had left in possession of my furniture and quarters; and I had not gone many yards towards the Convent-gate, when I met Doctor W. Durie and Captain Hughes, both of the Royal Artillery; upon which I expressed my satisfaction at having an opportunity of conferring with Hughes, with whom I had been at the Royal Military Academy at Woolwich. I had no sooner expressed my anxiety on the subject, than Hughes hung his head, and made no reply, which caused me to repeat the necessity I felt of discussing several points of military duty, which it was important should be immediately arranged; still, however, Hughes took no notice of me at all; but Durie said, " Don't speak to him."

"I must speak with him, and that, too, immediately," I retorted, impatiently. "We are going together on the expedition, and I have much to say to him."

"You cannot speak to him, he is not well," Durie hastily replied.

I was absolutely struck dumb with surprise, for Hughes had during that time remained with his eyes idiotically fixed on the ground, without moving a single muscle of his countenance, nor did he even appear to be conscious of what was passing.

Durie and Hughes walked on, and that was the last time I saw the latter.

I was afterwards informed, that on being appointed to take upon himself the command of the Royal Artillery attached to the troops under Spencer's division, he had become of unsound mind, frequently exclaiming that he could not support himself under responsibilities of such weight.

A few moments after I had parted with Durie and Hughes, I met Lieutenant-Colonel Bathurst, Chief of the Quarter-Master-General's department, who assured me that the General was exceedingly anxious to depart; and that we should either go that evening, or at an early hour on the following morning.

This short delay was very agreeable, for it gave us all an opportunity of providing little comforts, which are trifles on shore, but great conveniences, and almost necessities, at sea; it also enabled us to settle personally a number of pecuniary matters, instead of burthening our kind friends in attending to their settlement.

The appointment of Captain Morrison from the garrison of Gibraltar, to assume the command of the Royal Artillery in the place of Captain Hughes, was very agreeable to me; for, independently of our having been educated

MY MILITARY LIFE. 237

together at the Royal Military Academy at Woolwich, we had always remained on friendly terms. As Morrison was to embark on the same transport as myself, we now lost no time in making various arrangements of importance, both of a military and of a social interest. I then waited on Sir Hew Dalrymple, the Commander-in-Chief, to take leave; when his Excellency told me that we should, in the first instance, join the blockading fleet off Cadiz, and there receive further orders as to our destination.

Having completed my arrangements by four o'clock, I went to dine at the Engineers' mess; but either fatigue or over-excitement had totally robbed me of my appetite.

At five I rose from the table, when Mercer and I were accompanied by our brother officers to Ragged Staff, the place of embarcation, and on the way thither we were joined by Morrison and his friends, Lieutenant-Colonel G. Ramsay of the Artillery being one of the party. By half-past six o'clock P.M., the whole of the stores having been put on board, we shook hands with our friends, who heartily wished us every success in the services we might be engaged on; and as we pulled from the shore, they waved their hats thrice, but without cheering. This signal was, however, caught by a large number of officers, soldiers, and some ladies on the ramparts, at the top of the stairs, overlooking our movements, and they immediately saluted us with loud and enthusiastic cheers, in which we could not help joining; the troops in many ships re-echoed the huzzas, and these being answered by others more distant, this highly exciting demonstration of unspeakable feelings was rapidly taken up, from ship to ship, until it had completely gone the round of the whole fleet.

I had been incessantly and actively engaged from four o'clock in the morning up to this time; therefore, after settling such affairs as required immediate attention, I hastened to rest, in order that I might be prepared to enter upon the duties of the field, on the following day, in the event of our debarcation for the attack of Ceuta, on the opposite side of the Straits.

Our party consisted of Captain Morrison and Lieutenants Johnson and Festing of the Royal Artillery, and Lieutenant Mercer with myself of the Royal Engineers. I was the senior officer on board, and, consequently, took possession of the state cabin. In addition to the above, the Chaplain to the expedition was ordered to embark with us.

On the next day (14th of May), sometime before the morning gun had been fired, the signal for sailing was made; and as we were all desirous of taking another look at the rock, which might be the last, we hastened to the deck. I had been there but a short time, when I perceived with pleasure, Serjeant-Major Turner, of my company of Royal Military Artificers, coming to us from the shore, and he soon delivered to me several articles I had the previous evening requested my friend Harding to send me, particularly four large engraved views of Cadiz. I availed myself of this opportunity to despatch my servant to the town with the Serjeant-Major, in order to procure many trifles which we now discovered had been omitted in the sea stock. By eleven o'clock A.M. my servant had returned, and after much struggling with the baffling winds, we extricated ourselves from the bay.

To get a large number of ships under sail in the bay of Gibraltar, during an Easterly wind, is frequently attended with some difficulty, even for a single ship; and is always a work of time, since the steady and true course of the wind is obstructed by the proximity of the long and elevated rock, extending in a North and South direction, which causes the wind to drive round its two extremities, first on one side then on the other, and sometimes round both North and South at once, and thus reaches the shipping in strong gusts and flurries, forming numerous whirlwinds, running and crossing each other in contrary directions. I have known a ship of war, during an Easterly wind, to be four hours striving to get out of the Bay of Gibraltar, with five or six boats a-head, towing; and when a sufficient power of boats could not be applied, the practice has been to spread the fore-and-aft sails only.

CHAPTER XV.

Active speculations as to the destination of the expedition—Join the fleet off Cadiz—Sir John Gore fired upon, while carrying a flag of truce—General Spencer as Lieutenant-Colonel commanding the 40th Regiment on landing in Egypt—Frequent intercourse with the fishing boats—Profitable trade carried on off Cadiz—Catching whales no joke.

ALTHOUGH the secrecy observed in respect of our destination had frequently excited many surmises amongst us separately, yet our time had been so fully engaged in making the necessary arrangements for embarcation, that we had no opportunity of consulting each other on the subject, with a view of comparing notes and ideas, which might tend to guide us in adopting some opinion thereon.

But we had now abundance of leisure for speculating on our future movements. The slightest expressions or hints dropped by any of the big-wigs, about head-quarters, had been snapped at, and treasured up as so many keys to this important mystery ; each of the party had something of this sort to contribute to the general stock of information now collecting; some had absolutely heard the General say that it would be well to be at all times, and under all circumstances, ready to land the army ; another had been told that the Quarter-Master-General had objected to certain arrangements respecting the ammunition ; a third had formed his opinion that we must be going to the West Indies, from the knowledge he possessed of the nature of the medical stores: in short, one had jumped at an opinion that we were going to occupy the Azores, or Western Islands, but was unable to assign any motives whatever for this opinion. My information, which I had received direct from Sir Hew Dalrymple, was not only regarded as the most authentic, but every word which he had expressed was most carefully weighed and considered ; yet it helped us to no conclusion beyond the simple fact, that we should, in the first place, join the blockading squadron off Cadiz!

That we were going to the fleet seemed to be very probable, by our starting with an Easterly wind, and by the course we were then steering through the Straits of Gibraltar. But might this not be done, in order to conceal from the Spaniards an attack upon Ceuta, only sixteen miles distant from Gibraltar, and from which place all the movements of our expedition were perfectly visible? Might we not actually join the fleet, and immediately, during the night, run back to Ceuta, which the strong and constant current into the Mediterranean would render easy, notwithstanding the contrary wind from the Eastward?

All this appeared to be very reasonable, and quite consistent with military *ruse*. Whilst in the midst of these very conclusive calculations, we were informed by the master of the ship, that prior to our sailing, the whole of the transports had been victualled and watered for four months! This threw an entirely new light on our prospects. Why should we require provision for four months, if we were destined to attack Ceuta? Yet this also might be a trick to blind the enemy. We had not a sufficient force to make any attempt on Cadiz, but on reaching the fleet we might be reinforced by troops from England; still our means were quite adequate to capture some of the Spanish islands on the coast of Africa!

"No, no," maintained one of the party, "the four months' provision must be regarded as a convincing proof that we are bound to South America!"

In this way was passed a great portion of the day, our fleet drifting along through the Straits without anything worthy of notice, excepting that a brig, in keeping too near to the Spanish battery on Cabrista-Point, was frequently fired at, without, I believe, sustaining any injury.

By sunset we passed Cape Spartel, in Africa, and reached the open Atlantic. I was half sea-sick, and took no dinner, but remained on deck; the others were not quite so well, and went to bed. The wind sprang up, but the sky was clear; and at thirty-seven minutes past eight o'clock, as I was walking towards the head of the ship, a splendid meteor darted through the atmosphere from the South-east towards the North-west points of the compass, crossing in its transit the bows of our ship, upon which, without a moment's reflection, I hailed it as a favourable omen. This circumstance immediately brought to my recollection that the late General Köehler, of the Royal Artillery, had often related to me, when I was a child, that whilst attending as Aide-de-Camp on the celebrated General Elliot, Governor of Gibraltar (afterwards the first Lord Heathfield), at the sortie from Gibraltar (on the 27th of November, 1781), destined to destroy the works of attack carried on by the French and Spaniards during the late memorable siege, a meteor of this kind had crossed the General's path as he was passing out of the principal gate of the fortifications; upon which he also had made a similar exclamation, " I hail thee as a favourable omen!"

Before I proceed with an account of our most harassing cruise off the harbour of Cadiz, I must explain, that, although I may appear to have followed the entries made in my journal during that period in too much detail, yet as many of those notes, which may appear trivial, lead to other events of importance, I hope the reader will pardon my having done so.

As the night advanced the wind increased to a sort of gale, and by the morning of the following day we joined the blockading fleet off Cadiz; and we were so near to that famous city, as to be enabled, with the aid of my telescope, to distinguish many buildings in detail, and could distinguish windows that were open from those which were shut.

The extreme uncertainty, and consequent anxiety, we experienced, as to the service we might be destined to perform, together with the constantly tantalizing changes in our prospects, may be better and more briefly stated, by making a few extracts from my journal, which I now deeply regret was only kept during the first month of the time whilst I was embarked on this expeditionary service.

On the 15th of May, 1808, we joined the fleet off Cadiz, and from that moment followed its movements, that is, we stood towards the land during four hours, and then for four hours sailed in the contrary direction; and this was continued during the whole of the time we were with the fleet, excepting when at anchor.

On the 16th, in the evening, we hailed the Grasshopper, gun-brig, Captain Searle, to obtain a surgeon's attendance on one of the soldier's wives, about to add to the number of persons on board. Searle invited me to go on board his brig, when he informed me that Sir John Gore, commanding the Revenge, of seventy-four guns, had carried a flag of truce into Cadiz; and that we were all to be landed on the next day. This evening we could easily distinguish the tricoloured flags on board the French ships of war in the harbour from those of the Spaniards. I returned to my ship at seven o'clock, promising to dine with Searle the next day.

17th. A fine day, the Grasshopper about two miles distant; went to her, and arrived just in time, for the dinner was at that moment served: Captain Halstead, R.N., and Captain

Preston, General Spencer's aide-de-camp, were there also. It appears that Sir J. Gore, with his flag of truce, had been fired upon; but I could not learn whether it was from the batteries or the ships. On my way back to the transport I could distinctly hear the firing of heavy cannon, and several volleys of musketry. We obtained a good supply of fish to-day from the Spanish boats. At night there was much lightning.

In the course of our conversation after dinner, on board the Grasshopper, some one of the party inquired what service General Spencer had seen; upon which Preston related that the General, whilst a Lieutenant-Colonel, and commanding the 40th Regiment, had landed at the head of the first division of the army in Egypt, and was either actually the first man, or nearly so, who had jumped on the shore from the boats. The enemy on that occasion occupied a range of sand-hills closely following the margin of the sea, whence they kept up a galling fire from small arms and field artillery on the boats as they approached, in order to prevent, if possible, the debarcation of our troops. It was under these circumstances that this gallant officer leaped on to the sea-beach; upon which a French soldier instantly ran out from behind the sands, and advanced to within a short distance of him, took a deliberate aim at Spencer, and seemingly deprived him of any chance of escape. The Colonel, however, was not in the least degree dismayed, but immediately raised his cane, for he had not drawn his sword, and shaking it at the soldier, his eyes flashing ferociously at the same time, called out with a thundering voice, "Oh, you scoundrel!" Spencer's extraordinary composure under such desperate circumstances seems to have paralysed the Frenchman's intentions; for, without firing, he shouldered his musket with all possible expedition, and darted off to his comrades behind the sand-hills.

18th. The expectation raised in us the day before yesterday, that we should land forthwith, was totally destroyed on being informed this morning that Sir John Gore, in the Revenge, had been fired upon. Our spirits are, nevertheless, buoyed up, since there are so many movements in the fleet, and exchanges of communications. The French ships of war this morning got under-way, and ran up the harbour as far as they could; we can distinguish their colours, and they do not appear to be more than five or six miles distant.

I did not go on board the Grasshopper to meet Captain Preston, A.D.C., and Captain Halstead, R.N., as invited; she was too far off, and the wind, moreover, was very strong.

19th. The fishermen tell us that the French have possession of the batteries.

At daylight this morning we discovered that in the course of last night two merchant brigs and one ship had joined us, having, as usual, no other destination; and before midday another ship and a brig arrived, all from England or Ireland. I went on board the nearest of them, and purchased some pickles and sauces, a ham, and half-a-dozen of tooth brushes. Whilst I was on board there came alongside eleven Spanish fishing vessels, as they pretended to be, each from twenty to thirty tons burden. Our merchantmen came out laden with goods expressely assorted to supply the wants and tastes of both navy and army; but they also brought a much larger amount of other goods to be disposed of to traders or merchants who came in the feluchas expressly for that purpose, who were well acquainted with the manner of smuggling the goods into Spain without incurring the slightest risk. The merchant vessels always brought with them either the owners or agents, for the purpose of *selling-off* for hard cash on delivery; and, on this occasion, I saw seven thousand eight hundred and odd dollars counted out in twenties on the cabin table by one of the Spanish purchasers; the goods were at the same time hoisting out of the hold and shipping over the side into the feluchas. These goods consisted chiefly of the finest stationery and Manchester wares, particularly very fine cotton stockings, always in great demand among the Spanish ladies, and sure of being sold off most expeditiously; some ready-made cloth coats, boots and shoes, and round hats.

The goods destined for the military and navy in the fleet were chiefly Hessian boots and shoes, gentlemen's gloves, blue worsted elastic pantaloons, India handkerchiefs, a few cocked hats, and some fine pomatums, perfumes, combs, brushes of all sorts, blacking in great profusion; but without fail, a good lot of newspapers, and army lists, and Steele's navy lists. The papers were eagerly purchased at one shilling each. Hams, tongues, rounds of beef put into pickle on departure, and fresh butter in double casks, with brine between the two—potted meats, shrimps, cheese, porter, port-wine, pickled salmon, and plenty of potatoes—grocery of every description. The sales of the whole of these goods were effected so expeditiously, that I believe the five ships and brigs above mentioned were cleared out in five to six days; the proceeds all in hard cash had been paid, and off they were with all convenient speed, to return and dispose of another lading in a similar profitable manner; which, I was assured, amounted to thirty-five, and even double that per-centage on the cost. Of this, I was assured by a gentleman whom I afterwards met in England; and in conversing upon the profits he had himself realized in that way, he always closed by saying, "Oh, those were glorious times ! I cleared a very independent fortune in less than two years in that very trade; but, mind you, I always carried it on myself, and never through any of your confounded commission agents." It is indisputable, that under the very rare and peculiar circumstances of this trade, there could be none of the ordinary charges for lights, harbour dues, pilotage, wharfage, customs, warehousing, commission or agency, and, above all, pilferings and bad debts. I regret that I have no record of the number of vessels that profited by this very free trade during about twelve weeks we were off Cadiz with the blockading squadron. I had nearly forgotten to mention one of the sources of profit which these traders never neglected, that is, cashing the drafts or bills of officers of the army and navy; but they were exceedingly cautious, and many of us fancied they were too much so—moreover, the rate of exchange was always rather higher than at Gibraltar.

20th. At about five o'clock this morning my servant hurried into my cabin, exclaiming, there was an enormous whale sailing about the fleet, spouting up torrents of water, enough to sink any of the ships it might fall upon. I hastened upon deck just as a boat had been let down into the water, and found the skipper in a confusion of delight, making all the preparations necessary to give chase and secure the valuable prize; and having handed into the boat harpoons and coils of rope, or lines, as he called them, in vast abundance, together with several tubs for holding the same, and I know not how many other matters and things, amongst them a bran new coil of topgallant halyards. On noticing me, he asked me if I should like to have a taste of whale fishing. I cannot say I had any very pressing inclination to run the risk of being tossed up, boat and all, into the air; yet I cannot account for my having been so imprudent, for I accepted the invitation with as much pleasure as I might have experienced had it been to join in some favourite sport. There is no accounting for such mistakes.

Without looking behind me or sending a word of communication to any other officers on board, I went down into the boat in the fullest expectation of joining the breakfast party at the usual hour. It is very clear I had never before this had any thing to do with whale-fishing; but I placed my fullest confidence in our worthy skipper, an old and well reputed man in the whale-fishing seas. And, moreover, two of the boat's crew had also distinguished themselves in some of the Hull ships. "Shove off there!" and we started to seize on a one or two hundred-pounder fish, as sure as the North Star. Our master frequently repeated, "if we could but get a fair hold with the harpoon in the right place." We now dashed away in the direction in which the whale had been last seen; and to my extreme terror, he very soon rose to the surface within twenty feet of the boat, and instantly spouted such a stream of water as I then fully believed would have sunk us, had it unfortunately pitched into us. At this instant our commander, with extraordinary force and skill, darted the fatal harpoon deep into the monster, striking him just under one of his fins, which caused him to give a most convulsive and powerful flap with that fin on the surface of the water; and he plunged down almost vertically, producing such a commotion in the sea around us, that cascades were formed, diverging from the centre in every direction, and endangering our safety. Although by this time I had seen quite enough, and should have been glad to return to the transport, I held my peace, and suffered matters to adjust themselves mechanically, as a philosopher would say. The delighted skipper was now full of life and good spirits, and attended most anxiously to the clearing the line from the tubs in succession; and finding that the demand for more line went on unabated, he began to express some uneasiness lest the royal or top-gallant halyards should be absolutely required; for he had intended the piece of new rope to come into play towards the end of the game, yet away it began to run out whilst our crew were pulling with all their strength in the direction of the strain upon the line, in order to ease the jerk, should the fish not think proper to take breath before. At length the fish rose, evidently much exhausted, and having blown several times he went down again, and dragged the line after him much faster than we could row the boat; and having drawn out nearly the whole of the favourite halyards, the end being fastened to the boat, he pulled us away at such a rate that we all got into the stern to keep the bows above water. In this style we passed close to many of the transports in the fleet, and were cheered by them, and after many pauses inducing us to believe that our friend was rather sick of the fun; yet not before we had been dragged away latterly at a moderate rate, some ten to fifteen miles to the South-West of the fleet; and whilst we were very actively engaged in rowing on his track, and drawing in some of the line, the fish made a sudden start and instantly broke it, carrying away every inch that was beyond the gunwale of the boat. Oh! our poor skipper, how he did roar, how he lamented the loss of so much line, but very particularly the halyards, the bran-new halyards!! Night was now at hand, and we had a long pull to get back; we were all hungry as sharks, not a mouthful or a drop of fresh water had been put into the boat, and we might be caught in a gale, of which there seemed to be many indications. Consequently, without further lament we applied the remaining strength left amongst us, and worked hard at the oars, so that by midnight we had the good fortune to climb up the side of our excellent transport, where some biscuit and porter was all I could procure.

CHAPTER XVI.

Lord Amelius Beauclerk and his little Terrible—Cape Flyaway—The Spanish fishing boats—A row on board the Admiral—The author has a narrow escape of being shot in mistake.

21st. THE fishermen yesterday could not supply us with much provision; a few golden bream were procured, that is, eleven for four Spanish dollars. We are still without any orders to prepare for going on shore. For some days past we have been much amused by a miniature ship of the line, a complete model of the Terrible, commanded by Lord Amelius Beauclerk. She was, I was told, the launch of that ship, which had been fitted up with masts and sails, and rigging quite perfect; and she frequently went out managed by midshipmen, and when at a considerable distance from the big Terrible, signals were exchanged and telegraphing practised. On several occasions I have seen a boat full of Spanish gentlemen, and ladies too, board the Terrible, and for their amusement the little Terrible was telegraphed, and made to take in sail—to go on—to steer to this and that way—which was always done in compliance with the orders of one of the ladies, and obeyed without its being possible for them to discover by what means the orders had been conveyed a distance, sometimes a mile or two from the ship they were in.; but the signals were always, of course, necessarily made hanging from the stern instead of above the deck, and consequently, quite out of sight from the place where the company were stationed; and this was necessary in order to avoid any interference with the official signals of the fleet.

Just at the moment of the sun descending below the horizon, a large mass, resembling an abrupt rock was seen by all on board, and which was exactly betwixt us and the sun; and as soon as the sun had sunk totally, this unknown rock was no longer visible. We were at this time at anchor twenty-seven miles distant from Cadiz, and the stranger seemed to be, at least, fifty miles from us. The skipper declared he could not give any account of it, or claim any acquaintance with it; nor could he find even the vaguest notice of it on any of the maps and charts; we, therefore, came to the conclusion it must have been Cape Flyaway; and we never saw it afterwards.

On the 21st, having passed a number of hours in our boat, visiting the fishing vessels without being able to procure either news or eatables, we returned on board our floating mansion; and after dressing for dinner, I had just returned to the deck, when I perceived we were very close to Admiral Purvis's flag ship, not further, perhaps, than one hundred and fifty to two hundred yards. A signal was at this time made for the transports to go about and sail away in another direction; and it afterwards appeared that it was the duty of our skipper to be the first to obey the order; but he had delayed this longer than is usually allowed. I quickly heard the sound of a speaking trumpet from the flag-ship, expressing angry displeasure at the negligence ; but the object of it, our master had not clearly comprehended. The gentlemen of His Majesty's war ships are not always over-patient under such circumstances ; and, no doubt, they often had reason to complain of the delay in obeying an order. It was thus, our friend the officer of the watch on board the Admiral, felt he had great reason to insist, in a very peremptory manner, on proper respect being shown to the signal; and without pausing to consider, he adopted the usual course, which is, to fire a musket shot into the sails, or any where high above the after-part of a disobedient ship. I was calmly looking on, over the side of the transport, expecting, perhaps, to see our friend a shark dodging about, and at all that was passing, when I saw a Lieutenant standing up in a conspicuous manner above the hammocks with a musket in his hand, which he instantly pointed towards me, and as quickly let fly, when I distinctly heard the shot strike something just over my head. On turning round to find any mark it might have made, Captain Morrison, of the Artillery, at once pointed to the ball sticking in the boom about a foot above my head.

Many circumstances combined at that moment to fire my blood at this event; and, without a delay of five seconds, I snatched up a musket I had not long before charged with a ball, in order to fire at a large shark that had been all the morning sailing, as they say, about the ship. I instantly took a steady aim at the officer who had fired at me, and returned the compliment, lodging the ball, as afterwards ascertained in the hammocks just under his chin; and, in order that I might be the first to prefer my complaint, I jumped into the boat then alongside, and proceeded with all possible speed to the flag-ship, whilst, at the same time, an officer started thence to inquire into all the particulars of the cause of the insult which His Majesty's flag had thus sustained. The officer attempted to discuss the affair with me, as we met on the water in the boats; but I peremptorily declined it, observing, that I could not communicate on that subject with any body but my own commanding-officer, General Spencer. I, therefore, proceeded; and, on reaching the deck, I was met by Spencer and Purvis, both regarding me with an air of unmistakeable severity. Saluting the Admiral with a full drop of my hat, which, however, his offended dignity scarcely permitted him to notice, I bowed to the General, and advanced with that bold and firm step belonging to an injured person seeking for redress, I at once announced that the object of my visit was to seek his Excellency's protection and interference, in order to obtain redress for the violent outrage which had been committed on me, by some person on board the flag-ship, who had fired a shot directly at me, and, I might have added, " and no mistake," with no other object, that I could discover, but that of murdering me, and that, too, without any discoverable cause or provocation on my part.

The Admiral, with whom I was on friendly terms, regarded me whilst I was addressing the General, with a sort of smile or sneer of contempt; and soon interrupted me, by saying to the General, "This officer must be under some strange delusion. I am anxious to learn how he will excuse himself for having insulted His Majesty's flag in a most unheard-of manner; for, as to the tale about an officer in my ship having, in the wanton way he has asserted, attempted to murder him, that can be very soon set at rest, by the report of the officer I sent on board the transport." Purvis then turned upon his heel, and walked away to the other end of the quarter-deck.

Spencer now drew me away in the contrary direction, and said,—" I am very much afraid you will find this affair to be far more serious than you seem to expect. The act of violence you have committed towards the flag, and especially towards the officer who fired the musket into the rigging or sails of your transport, you will find to be a very difficult and complicated offence to explain in a satisfactory manner."

The Admiral, manifesting a considerable degree of impatience at the delay in the return of the officer, came up, and addressing me, evidently in no very pleasant temper, but which his gentlemanly feelings struggled to conceal, he said,—" Pray, sir, have the goodness to tell me on what grounds do you suppose my officer intended to murder you, as you have asserted?"

I then at once said, " Sir, the shot fired at me, or of which I have to complain, is now sticking in the boom of the fore-and-aft main-sail of my transport, scarcely, at the time, one foot from my head." The Admiral at this cast a very anxious look at Spencer, when I continued : " From which circumstance I did at the moment believe it had been fired at me, and my feelings were greatly excited, as it brought back to my mind, in the most painful manner, the affliction I not long since suffered through the death of my dear and intimate friend, Captain Bains, of the 6th Regiment of Foot, whose head was shot off, when crossing the channel to Jersey or Guernsey in a packet, by a cannon-ball fired at that vessel, by one of His Majesty's ships of war, for not obeying some signal; but, of course, in which the Captain, my friend, could have had no authority to prevent, or incur any blame for the neglect of the master of the packet. This circumstance has ever since been fresh before my eyes, and may, and probably did, increase the irritation I was under at the time. I fired at the individual who had first fired, as I fully thought at me, for I cannot for a moment suppose that any man could really intend to fire into the upper sails or rigging of a ship so near him, and strike the boom in mistake; if so, he must be a very unfit person to be intrusted with the discharge of a duty so delicate, and of such a nature that, by committing a blunder or mistake like that, he might take away the life of an innocent person."

My explanation had rather the effect of augmenting the Admiral's displeasure, whilst Spencer stood by with his never-failing composure, and observed,

"The boat is just coming alongside with the officer, whose report will, I hope, satisfactorily explain this complicated affair."

The Admiral added, "I hope so too, General, but I scarcely think it possible."

The officer was on deck in an instant; and, advancing to the Admiral, wished to make his report to him separately, but Purvis exclaimed, "Speak out, sir, whatever you have to say; the insult was public enough, the report you have to make must be as public;" upon which the officer at once said,—

"In compliance with your orders, Admiral, I went on board of the transport (287), which had disobeyed orders, and at which you had ordered a musket-shot to be fired in the upper rigging."

"Well, sir;" the impatience of the Admiral momentarily increasing. "Well, sir," he repeated, "tell us at once what is the information you obtained."

"Sir, all hands agreed that a ball pointed out to me, and now sticking in the boom of the vessel, on that side that had been towards us at the time, had actually been fired from this ship, and that the officer here present was standing, so that it must have passed within a few inches of the top of his head. I have here," drawing out his pocket-book, "the names of all the officers and other witnesses who are ready to give evidence to that effect if required;" at the same time handing to the

MY MILITARY LIFE. 269

Admiral the names of Captain Morrison commanding the Artillery, Lieutenant Mercer of the Royal Engineers, and of several of the soldiers of Artillery, and of some of the seamen.

During the time the officer was making his report, I had carefully observed the General's countenance with deep interest, but I could not notice the slightest alteration, whilst the colour of the Admiral's had several times reddened and faded. Purvis did not speak, and was evidently not only perplexed, but, I should say, somewhat disappointed. After a few seconds, without expressing any opinion, he took Spencer's arm, and they walked away and entered the cabin, but soon after sallied forth again, every one of us who had been present at the delivery of the report having remained exactly in the same place, and, I believe, without exchanging a single word with any one, all, no doubt, speculating on the *dénouement*. In about five minutes we saw the two chiefs returning from their consultation, when the most perfect silence prevailed, even the gentle sea-breeze, which had been playing about the rigging and royals, was hushed.

After the pause of two or three seconds, the Admiral, with a slight nervous agitation of manner, said, it appeared to both the General and himself that we were each of us equally to blame; the officer of the navy had certainly fired a shot in a very incautious way, by which the life of the officer commanding the Engineers, serving under General Spencer, had been somewhat endangered, but that it was past all doubt without any intention of terminating his life; yet his conduct was by no means free from blame on that account, but was clearly highly reprehensible. With regard to the officer of the land service, who had, by his own admission, deliberately fired at the officer of the navy whilst in the discharge of his duty; he felt convinced that had there not, unfortunately, been a loaded musket almost in his hands at the time, he would not have sought further to procure that means of retaliation which must have caused sufficient delay to allow a relaxation of those feelings which had urged him to fire at any man with a desire of depriving him of his life, particularly when redress was so near at hand, without such violence. Reviewing all the circumstances of the case, the General as well as himself had come to the conclusion that no further proceedings would be necessary, that each party seemed to be equally culpable; the officer of the navy had directed his fire in a most careless and exceedingly improper manner, whilst the military officer had assumed that a state of things existed which was quite irreconcileable after a moment's reflection, and had acted upon it in a most rash and inconsiderate way. Fortunately, however, for the satisfaction of both services, no blood had been spilt; and he most sincerely hoped that we should follow the united advice of the General and himself, by shaking hands, and by forgetting the event. The advice was cheerfully adopted, and we both dined with the Admiral, drank wine together, and with every one at table, shook hands again, and parted. I never have seen him since, and I have now no recollection of his name.

CHAPTER XVII.

Prayers by the Chaplain—Flags of Truce—Mr. Collison—Captain Maxwell—Come to Anchor—Anxiety in regard to our Prospects—Conflicting Information—Signal for Adjutants—A Big Bundle of Boards—Our Skipper in a Stew—Go to Sea again—John Bull—Off towards Gibraltar—All our Hopes crushed—Recalled and sent back to the Fleet—Expectation of Disembarking—Disappointment—Anniversary of the Birth of George the Third—Sir John Gore and Sir George Smith—Marquis of Solana.

22ND. BEING Sunday, I insisted on the Chaplain reading prayers, which he had resisted as much as he was able; and we afterwards heard that General Spencer was gone to the mouth of the harbour of Cadiz, to be more conveniently placed to receive and reply to some flags of truce that had been passing all the morning; and we also learnt the melancholy death of Captain Hughes of the Artillery, whom we had left at Gibraltar.

On the 23rd we boarded the fishing boats, and only obtained a little bread and large onions. At midday a signal was made for transports to collect closer together, and soon after that we passed under the stern of the Alceste, Captain Maxwell, in order to speak. We were the nearest and first hailed, when the Captain said he should very soon come to anchor, and ordered us to do the same, at the distance of three cables' length to windward of him. We went on close to the wind; but I was much surprised on perceiving that the blockading ships remained cruizing. We passed within about four miles of Cadiz, and there we observed four English ships of the line at anchor, just out of reach of the batteries.

We anchored at about six miles from Cadiz, in twenty fathoms water, wind North-west by North, at seven o'clock P.M.

Our present state of uncertainty is again very vexatious; every movement assures us that a debarcation is at hand. By this time to-morrow we may have landed, and may have had a severe engagement; many of us may be under the sod, or may have been sunk in boats and drowned, or perhaps lying on the beach severely wounded; but we may be on our way back to Gibraltar, without having accomplished, or even attempted anything; and we may be here, as we now are, at anchor, without having made the least progress in unravelling the mystery as to our future movements.

Amidst such various and speculative chances, we must not, however, lose sight of this fact, that unless the people of Cadiz were amicably disposed towards us, our small force could not effect a landing; and our anchoring to windward of the entrance of the harbour would indicate that some arrangements are either made or expected to be completed, which will cause us to be landed on friendly terms with the Spaniards. Moreover, all the fishermen, with whom we daily converse, assure us that none of the French are allowed to leave their ships. From this it may be fairly conjectured that some revolution in the political relations betwixt them and the Spaniards, has already actually taken place; and, it appears to me, that any such change must terminate in uniting the interests of Spain and Britain against France.

It is, therefore, not unlikely that our fleet will be permitted to enter the harbour, in order to capture the French ships; whilst, as a proper guarantee, our troops will be put in possession of all the batteries that could fire on our fleet during its passage through the harbour.

24th. My mind being completely worn out with thinking, and my eyes sore in consequence of the almost incessant use I had made of the telescope, at a late hour last night I endeavoured to procure some repose; but instead of sleep, so deeply impressed was I that this day was to be one of great importance, and full of adventure, I could take no rest. At length my head ached violently, and I became very feverish; at six o'clock I rose, and went upon deck unrefreshed and more wearied, in every respect, than I had been on going to bed.

Time never crept on more heavily than on the present occasion; my watch, I thought, must be out of repair, or had not been wound up. After walking up and down until quite exhausted, instead of being summoned to dinner or supper, as I, perhaps, expected, it was only to breakfast.

Having made a hasty meal, I hurried off to the deck, when I had the inexpressible gratification of seeing a signal made on board a ship of war. "That must be," thought I, " to hoist out the boats, and prepare to land ;" yet it turned out to be for all Adjutants to attend on board the Alceste.

Accordingly, Festing of the Artillery, and Mercer of the Engineers, hastened to that ship. My glass was now constantly fixed on the Alceste, to catch the first display of the signal for all commanding officers. In vain I strained my sight; the two Adjutants returned, bringing with them nothing but a string of orders, relating to precautionary measures whilst at anchor ; such as mounting an officer's guard, and planting four sentinels in each ship, with orders to challenge every boat that might approach during the night. Thus, all our expectations of splendid achievements, which our sanguine dreams had put down to be realized on this very day, were in one instant totally destroyed; and in this way, from day to day, our hope had been raised and as quickly crushed.

On the 26th, towards sun-set, the wind augmented to a gale when, at about ten o'clock P.M., a large ship exactly to windward, began to drag her anchor, which compelled us to pay out the whole of our cable, in order to avoid being struck by her; this annoyed our skipper very much, and he went on muttering all kinds of abuse against both captain and ship; when, at length, observing that this enormous mass, still kept on steadily driving upon us, and no longer able to suppress his rage and contempt, he snatched up the speaking-trumpet, and with all the power of his lungs, hallooed out, " Hulloa there! you great, big bundle of boards; where are you coming to?" These words had scarcely reached their destination, when a thundering voice retorted, "What's that you say, you d—d rascally skipper? I'll have you on board here in a trice, and give you a couple of dozen, you lubber;—how dare you hail a man-of-war in that way?"

In an instant our crest-fallen-skipper's eyes were opened to his mistake and danger; for he now recollected that this great, big bundle of boards were nothing less than His Majesty's ship Batavia, an old forty-four gun-ship on two decks, having the 29th Regiment on board. He, therefore, dropped his elevated tone, and, in the most humble and supplicating expressions, prayed for forgiveness, which procured him a few more hearty curses, and a warning that the next offence would not be so easily overlooked.

In a few minutes afterwards, we narrowly escaped being run down by this ugly hen-house, as our master grumbled out, modifying the sound of his voice, so that none could clearly hear but those within a whispering distance, for she actually passed within a very few yards of our starboard side, fortunately without coming in contact. I recollect that

I thought at the time, our Captain was, perhaps, not entirely wrong, when he said to me, "They don't care about running us down; you see they have not done a single thing to prevent it;" he then explained all he thought the Batavia should have done, but of the merits of which I am no judge.

On the 27th, we weighed anchor, and stood out to sea, and, by the next morning, were completely out of sight of land, and, also, of the blockading fleet, the wind blowing hard, and steering W.N.W. Our conjectures were now again busily at work; nothing seemed to us more reasonable than a trip to Madeira, the West Indies, or South America; for it was clearly past a doubt that we were off from the coast of Europe; yet, after putting our minds to the rack for three or four hours, a signal was made to go about, and, in the course of the evening, we found ourselves again with the fleet, and within sight of the city of Cadiz.

On the 30th, we ran in close to Cadiz, and, at twelve o'clock, the Spaniards fired a royal salute; but I could not learn the cause.

On the 31st, we observed the Aukland brig, post-office packet, commanded by Captain John Bull. I immediately prepared two letters, whilst Festing went on board, and, on his return, acquainted us that the Admiral had told Captain Bull that we were all to return to Gibraltar to-morrow. But this measure was ordered to be carried into effect immediately, for, in less than an hour, the convoying frigates and brigs led the way, directing their course towards the Straits of Gibraltar; and the whole of the troop-ships obeyed, crowding all sail: in passing close to one of the frigates, I could distinguish General Spencer and staff, on board of her.

"Now," thought I, " our expedition is certainly at an end;" and so every one else on board of the fleet had considered it; yet we were again deceived, for we had not proceeded a single mile, when signals were seen flying from the masts of every man-of-war; and, immediately afterwards, with crowded sails they were running direct towards Cadiz; the whole of the transports following them with the utmost alacrity.

Just before this, we had observed a seventy-four gun ship, near the harbour, displaying a succession of signals, firing guns, and hastening towards the fleet under as much canvass as she could spread.

Our recall had immediately followed; and in a couple of hours we had again reached that portion of the sea, which, if ships could mark the water as a plough does the land, would have presented a surface so intersected with tracks that, probably, not one square yard could have been found free from their crossings.

It being now five o'clock P.M., and at about seven or eight miles from Cadiz, we observed nearer in shore a seventy-four gun ship, with a white flag at the fore-top-gallant mast-head, and about the same time, the whole of the men-of-war lying-to hoisted their ensigns and pendants, the Admiral displaying his flag. "What can all this mean?" was the exclamation of every one.

Nothing could be more tantalizing than such a situation. My anxiety of mind was excessive; the perplexing confusion of ideas occasioned by the passing before my eyes of so many unexplained movements, was such, that I could not seize on any one probability, to serve as a nucleus round which to form some kind of opinion or conjecture as to the meaning of all this dumb show.

After an hour or two, we proceeded, and anchored at about three miles and a half from Cadiz, wind West North-west.

During the remainder of the daylight, several white flags were exchanged, and everything again assumed an air of business.

* Full of expectation that on the morrow we should be allowed to land, we retired to our beds.

1st of June. We were on the alert, and actively occupied in examining our pistols, putting in new flints, casting bullets, sharpening swords, fastening every button on our clothes, &c.

Morrison was up at an early hour, examining the state of the guns, and arranging everything, so as to be ready to land with the least trouble, confusion, or delay.

At ten o'clock a signal was made for all adjutants to attend and receive orders. This summons was always obeyed with alacrity, and upon the same principle as the postman's double tap produces an accelerated movement towards the house door; and although it was impossible that we could expect those (of the Artillery and Engineers) to return in less than an hour and a half, yet before the expiration of half that time we felt assured that they must be loitering on board much longer than was necessary. By the time when they returned, our impatience to learn all the interesting details for landing was excessive; but at length they ascended the deck, with faces neither more nor less cheerful than usual, and stated that the signal had been made at the request of Lieutenant-Colonel the Honourable George Lake, of the 29th Regiment, in order to apprise the troops that, as it was likely we should land either this day or the next morning, it was desirable that we should cook one or two days' provision.

2nd. Again disappointed, since no orders

for disembarking have as yet been given; however, white flags are still passing from side to side, and the ships of war are somewhat nearer to Cadiz. Our debarcation cannot be postponed beyond to-morrow.

3rd. This day was not productive of any new feature; although grievously disappointed, our hope was not altogether destroyed. We obtained ample supplies of fruits and vegetables from the Spanish fishing boats.

4th. This day being the anniversary of the King's birthday (George the Third), the ships at anchor were in full dress; that is, with the flags of every nation, and those used for signals, hoisted in regular order, from the deck to the highest points of the masts. Towards the middle of the day, the blockading fleet ran in much closer than usual, and lying to at twelve o'clock, they each of them fired a royal salute; the Admiral with the royal-standard at the main, and the fleet with colours and pendants hoisted. About this time I observed many boats filled with ladies and gentlemen from the shore sailing about us without fear, which indicated that hostilities were regarded as having terminated; and I saw one very large boat, called a falucha, containing several white friars, run alongside a ship at anchor very near us, and the passengers accepted an invitation to go on board.

5th. Being Sunday, we had prayers by the Chaplain : the wind was blowing strong, which made it difficult for the men to preserve line, or even to stand without holding on.

Yesterday evening we killed our last pig ; we, therefore, consider ourselves fortunate in having been able to procure two sheep for a doubloon (then worth four pounds), from a Spanish boat from Rota, and from the fishermen we heard that Sir John Gore and Colonel Sir George Smith are on shore at Cadiz, making arrangements for our landing. Through the same medium we are informed that the Marquis of Solano, Governor of Cadiz, was murdered by the populace on the 28th *ultimo*, because it was discovered he was totally devoted to the French party. He is reported to have been cut into small pieces by the mob, which were burnt in various parts of the city. The above is, however, but a fisherman's account.

MY MILITARY LIFE. 287

CHAPTER XVIII.

The ships of War anchor outside of the Transports—The Alceste goes to England with some Officers of the English and Spanish Armies—Lord Collingwood invites me to Dinner—Midshipman Festing dines at the Admiral's table also—Lord Collingwood's wit— General Spencer—I go on Shore, well received—I meet some old Friends—I receive some very kind presents of Provision—The Attack of the Ships belonging to Villeneuve's Squadron is commenced—The San José suffers no injury—The San José disabled—I go to Fort Luis—I am sent for by the Spanish Admiral, and requested to go to Collingwood for Powder —The 6th Regiment and some Artillery arrive from Gibraltar—The Spanish Officers account for not sinking the French Ships.

6TH. THE ships of the line came to anchor, forming an irregular crescent outside the transports. We now heard that the Alceste was about to sail for England; I, therefore, prepared some official and private letters, which I sent on board, and on the Adjutant's return, by whom I had sent them, we learnt that Lieutenant-Colonel Tucker, of the Adjutant-General's department, and two Spaniards, were to go to England in this ship. It was also again reported, that if the French ships did not very soon come out or surrender, possession of the batteries would be given to the British troops, whilst the fleet engaged them in the harbour. Another piece of news was, that the Spaniards had been refused an armistice for six months, which they had demanded.

In the course of the afternoon, it was rumoured that Captain Dalrymple, son of the Lieutenant-Governor of Gibraltar, and a Lieutenant or a Captain Tucker, had arrived from Gibraltar overland, and had gone on to Sevilla, there to attend a general council (*Junta Central*), appointed to determine on the course which it would be most expedient for that portion of Spain to follow which was still unoccupied by the French armies. Sir George Smith was reported to be living on shore in good style.

8th. Our patience was now so completely exhausted, that I resolved on paying a visit to the General on board Lord Collingwood's flagship, under a hope of gathering some clue to our prospects. The General received me with his usual cold politeness, and soon after my arrival on board, took me aside on the quarter-deck, and told me as a sort of secret, that the Spaniards had determined to commence their long-meditated attack on the five French ships of the line, and one frigate, on the following day, by opening a severe fire from all the batteries and gun-boats; but that none of the ships were to take any part in the attack, as it was supposed, after a "good cannonading," as the General expressed himself, the fleet would be surrendered. I then asked the General if there was any British officer on shore to report to him or to the Admiral; when Spencer looked very serious and silent, and made me no reply; but addressing Lieutenant-Colonel Tucker, said,—

"Under the circumstances, which you know, it certainly would be very desirable."

Upon this, without hesitation, I said, "that as it seemed the Spaniards were virtually at war with the French, they were, by that fact, at peace with the English, therefore there could be no objection to such a measure." Thus, whilst Spencer was revolving the subject in his mind, I added, "I should gladly obey an order to go on shore for that purpose. As to the objections the Spaniards might raise to that course, I felt no anxiety."

Spencer looked at Tucker inquisitively, and slightly disposed to smile; then turning to me, said, "There may be more danger in it than you seem to anticipate, Captain Landmann ;" but Tucker made some observation to the General I did not quite catch; which, however, induced Spencer to observe, "I consider it would be desirable."

The General having laid some emphasis on the last word, I replied, "Would your Excellency treat me as a deserter if I were to go on shore without an order ? the sea is exceedingly smooth," said I, "and I could land there," pointing to the outside of the fortifications of the Land Port of Cadiz; "if I only understood your Excellency did not forbid it. Once on shore, I should soon get myself into a battery or gun-boat, or some other place, where I should be able to make my notes for a report to your Excellency."

Spencer smiled, but did not speak.

I afterwards understood Colonel Sir George Smith, a man suffering much from ill health, with his head tied up in a black silk handkerchief, was on shore; and it was, perhaps, to him the General alluded. If it were true that Sir George was on shore, I am at a loss to assign any reason for the General's apparent difficulty about sending me on shore also. An officer, in whose judgment the General seemed to place much confidence, but who was unknown to me, and had joined us, soon after the commencement of our conversation, now took the General aside, and I distinctly heard him say,—

"Why not let him go on shore? you need not take any responsibility in the result."

Much more passed between them, when Tucker observed,—

"You'll go, I see; from the General's manner he wishes you to go, but does not like to give an order; why, I cannot understand."

At this moment the Admiral's dinner was ready, and I was about to ask the General if he had any further commands, for I had completely made up my mind to go on shore without saying another word to the General on the subject, having mentioned my intention to Tucker, who said,—

"I am glad you have guessed Spencer's wishes."

Lord Collingwood then politely said to me, "We are just going to dinner, sir; I shall be happy of your company, Captain ———. What is your name, sir?" I told his Lordship my name. "Very good—very good, sir;" and we sat down to dinner.

According to the usage, the Midshipman of the watch—always dressed on board the Ocean with blue breeches, white cotton stockings, and full gold-laced hat—was invited to dinner. The name of this Midshipman was Festing, a brother of my worthy friend Lieutenant Festing, of the Royal Artillery, who was embarked in the same transport as myself. I had often heard of Lord Collingwood's odd expressions. I, therefore, was upon the look-out; but the only thing worthy of being repeated was, on Festing being helped to a plate of soup, his Lordship said, "I say, youngster, swallow up that soup like soap-suds down a sink-hole."

As soon as the dinner was over, I took leave of the Admiral and of the General, who smiled as I left him, a rather unusual event with his Excellency, a man of the gravest, sternest, and most formal manners; indeed, so unbending was Spencer, that some five or six years after this period, I met him at the table of my worthy and excellent friend Lieutenant-General Sir Thomas Dyer, my neighbour in Clarges Street, of whom I have already had occasion to make mention, when Dyer told me, Spencer was so stiff and formal, that even his own brother did not venture to address him by his Christian name, Brent, as brothers are wont to practise, but always by his family name and rank prefixed.

Tucker accompanied me to the gang-way, and cautiously made no allusion to my going on shore, but observed,

" You speak Spanish very well, I believe ?"

" O yes, moderately; sufficient for ordinary purposes," said I.

" You will find it of great advantage," giving me a hearty shake of the hand; and with a significant look, said,—" We still have three hours' day-light, and a dead calm, pleasant time of it."

" Farewell," I replied, and away I pushed off, direct for the shore, only about three miles distant, when I immediately noticed the General and many others looking over the side of the ship at my movements. As I neared the beach, which is shallow, and in some places rocky, I perceived there was some surf breaking; but after a little shifting, and a good deal of management, we accomplished a landing, about a mile and a half from the city. I was met by several gentlemen, who advanced in a most friendly manner, holding out their arms, and embracing me with marks of extraordinary satisfaction; but on discovering I could explain myself in the Spanish language, their joy and delight were very great.

I lost no time in ordering the boat to return to the transport, and to acquaint Morrison where I was, and that I should not return on board so long as the tricoloured flags remained hoisted on the French ships. Some of the persons I had met on the beach, were very pressing that I should enter a light carriage which had brought them from Cadiz, and assured me I should be received with every possible attention, and they would provide a lodging with them. Upon this, I thanked them for their civility, but added, I had come on shore for business and not for pleasure, and I begged they would enable me to reach one of the forts, or any of the gun-boats destined to attack the French ship on the following day.

At this announcement they were overjoyed, for they assured me they were totally ignorant of the intention of any proceedings of that nature; and instantly yielding to my request, they conducted me in their carriage to Fort

Puntalis, where the Commandant received me with much civility, but added, he could not give me a place in the fort without some official authority. One of the gentlemen who had brought me to the fort proposed setting off with the carriage at full speed to Cadiz, to procure the Governor's order; and just as the carriage was about to set off for that purpose, I noticed an officer of the Spanish navy, who had just landed from his gun boat, near Puntales, and was advancing towards me, attracted by the novelty of seeing an English uniform amongst his friends outside of the fort. What must have been my surprise on holding folded in my arms my friend Don —— Cortasar, whom I had known in England some four or five years before, when Cortasar was a prisoner of war; as he had been captured on board the Fama, one of the four frigates taken off Cape St. Mary, on their return from South America, laden with treasure. My friend Cortasar, and all his brother officers, had experienced every civility and attention at my house in Gosport, in 1803. I was additionally surprised on hearing that

Don Francisco Carrillo, another of the officers of the Fama, was also at Cadiz, and both of them at that moment commanding gun-boats, preparing for the attack on the French ships; Cortasar immediately took me on board his gun-boat, and having sent for Carrillo, whose astonishment at seeing me so unexpectedly cannot be described, we passed the evening together on humble fare, and at midnight I rolled myself up in a Spanish cloak on the deck, and slept soundly. Carrillo returned to his boat, but was with us soon after daylight, when a messenger and assistant arrived from Cadiz, laden with a considerable quantity of cooked ham, fowls, wine and fruits, as a present for me; but I never learnt to whom I was indebted for this very kind attention, the messenger constantly refusing to disclose the name of the gentleman who had employed him. We all three sat down to this splendid repast, and had scarcely finished, when an officer came in a fast boat, and brought Cortasar instructions to hold the boat ready for action; and that a red flag at the main of the Admiral's ship in the outer harbour, would be the signal for commencing business. Very punctually, at three o'clock in the afternoon, the much-desired signal was made; and within five seconds after, every gun-boat, every gun and mortar on shore, had fired at the French ships; and, I believe, that in less time than twenty seconds every gun on board the French ships had returned the compliment. The explosions of the guns, mortars, and bursting of shells was, I should think, without parallel. In this manner the thundering of ordnance went on at the rate of two hundred to three hundred per minute, until about eight o'clock at night, when it was almost totally suspended. During about the first two hours from the commencement of the action, our boat, the San José, seemed to have altogether escaped the notice of the enemy; which was somewhat curious, for the whole of the gun-boats were judiciously scattered, in order to divide the fire from the ships; and in that time we had pointed our twenty-six pounder with the calmest deliberation, without being recognized by the enemy, for I could not say that one shot had been directed at us individually. However, one of the ships at length perceived we seemed to have it all our own way, and industriously gave us the benefit of her fire. Her shot rattled over, some under, some to the right, others to the left, but not one came sufficiently near our boat, the celebrated San José, to be regarded as a narrow escape, leaving us at eight o'clock at night, when the firing ceased on all sides, with every rope and gear as whole and unhurt as on our going into action; and the ships also, notwithstanding the enormous expenditure of ammunition, as far as we could judge, had suffered but little damage!

Carrillo now joined us, and his boat likewise had been but slightly injured in the rigging. He brought with him two other officers from the boats, about ten of which had fallen back, and lay in a cluster near Puntales; and as I had again received a second supply from the liberality of my unknown friend in town, we made merry and amused ourselves until a late hour. In the course of our conversation, I had the pleasure of hearing that one of their companions in the Fama, Lieutenant Chacon, a little Biscayan, had been promoted; and that Howdrigue had retired from the service, and had inherited a good fortune. Chacon was exceedingly diminutive in person, very dark in colour, and one of the liveliest possible companions.

10th. Exactly at eight o'clock in the morning, the red flag was again displayed at the main of the Spanish admiral's ship, the signal for renewing the action. The cannonading was now just as hot as it had been on the preceding day; but the San José had become the favourite target for the enemy. Two of their ships having given us a few broadsides, we sustained some severe injuries; but the worst of all was a shot which struck us in the bows, a foot or more below the water-line, and rendered it necessary to run back the gun, and keep as many of the people on board quite in the stern, to raise the bow out of water, whilst a row-boat towed us into shallow water near Fort Puntales. The San José being thus disabled, I procured a passage in a man-of-war's boat going over to Fort Louis. The enemy, I could here observe, had adopted a good plan for injuring the gun-boats, which was to concentrate their fire upon one at a time, by which means two of them were very soon sunk, and the crews narrowly escaped being drowned, by the timely arrival of their friends. From Fort Louis I had a much better view of the operations. Here the ships had done some mischief; a few men had been killed and wounded, and had been removed, I believed, to Cadiz. At Fort Louis I experienced the utmost kindness, and shared the Commandant's meals with him, and passed the nights at his quarters, with some of the merriest fellows; one in particular, a Lieutenant from the flag-ship: he squinted very much, and was, perhaps, somewhat high-shouldered, but he related many of his adventures at Lima, and other parts of South America, with so much fun and quaintness, that daylight broke in upon us before we had suspected the lateness of the hour.

11th. Again, at the same hour, a similar signal produced a repetition of the bombardment and cannonading, not quite so well kept up; and the masts and yards seemed to have suffered very little. Our (Spanish) gunboats, about twenty-five or thirty in number, had escaped miraculously; only three of them had been sunk, and, as far as I was able to discover, there were not more than fifteen to twenty men killed, and thirty to forty wounded. I never learnt the amount of losses sustained by the enemy, excepting that only two of the shells had struck them. In the course of the afternoon, my presence at Fort Louis having been reported to the Admiral, he sent a boat with a letter for me to go to him on board his ship; when he stated the quantity of ammunition expended was so great, that he was under the necessity of applying to Lord Collingwood for a supply; he said, that twelve hundred of the largest shells had been fired at the enemy, and that now he could not renew the attack on the ships with spirit unless the British Admiral would supply him with three hundred barrels of gunpowder. He, therefore, requested that I would proceed to Lord Collingwood with a Spanish officer he should send with me, and represent the necessity of a compliance with his request. I lost not a moment in taking leave of the Admiral, and with a Spanish officer proceeded to the British Admiral. General Spencer received me very kindly, and having delivered the letter from the Spanish Admiral, with which I had been charged, addressed to Lord Collingwood, I was supplied with writing materials, and made my report to Spencer. After which a boat was ordered to convey me back to my transport, for I was tolerably worn out; but I do not know to this day if either the General or the Admiral made mention of me in any way in their correspondence.

Morrison and myself had been frequently present at the proving of the iron cannon in the Arsenal at Woolwich, on those occasions, when from one hundred to one hundred and fifty cannon were discharged in the short space of a couple of minutes, and these events had made a deep impression on our minds. Availing ourselves of that experience, we were agreed in adopting as a fact that the number of explosions of all sorts, and from all quarters, could not have been fewer than three hundred to three hundred and fifty during the first minute; and that during the first three hours they must have amounted to one hundred per minute.

I was informed that the 6th Regiment, and a detachment of the Royal Artillery, had joined us on the 10th.

In the following year, when at Cadiz, in conversing with the Spaniards on this subject, I expressed great surprise at the little damage sustained by the French ships; upon which they one and all invariably replied, that as they were sure of capturing the ships, they did not wish to injure them; indeed, they said, orders had been given to direct the fire over their decks. Moreover, they added, if we had sunk those large ships, which they might have done very easily, or have burnt them, they would have choked up the narrow channel in which they had anchored, the only one leading to the Carracas, or dock-yard.

END OF VOL. I.

www.ingramcontent.com/pod-product-compliance
Lightning Source LLC
Chambersburg PA
CBHW060832190426
43197CB00039B/2561